D0727461

WELL-BEING

PATRICIA FURNESS-SMITH

A PRACTICAL GUIDE

79 713 531 5

Published in the UK and USA
in 2015 by Icon Books Ltd,
Omnibus Business Centre,
39–41 North Road,
London N7 9DP
email: info@iconbooks.com
www.iconbooks.com

Sold in the UK, Europe and Asia
by Faber & Faber Ltd,
Bloomsbury House,
74–77 Great Russell Street,
London WC1B 3DA
or their agents

Distributed in South Africa
by Jonathan Ball,
Office B4, The District,
41 Sir Lowry Road,
Woodstock 7925

Distributed in Australia and
New Zealand
by Allen & Unwin Pty Ltd,
PO Box 8500,
83 Alexander Street,
Crows Nest,
NSW 2065

Distributed in Canada
by Publishers Group Canada,
76 Stafford Street, Unit 300
Toronto, Ontario M6J 2S1

Distributed to the trade in the USA
by Consortium Book Sales
and Distribution
The Keg House,
34 Thirteenth Avenue NE,
Suite 101,
Minneapolis, MN 55413-1007

ISBN: 978-184831-796-3

Text copyright © 2015 Patricia Furness-Smith

The author has asserted her moral rights.

No part of this book may be reproduced in any form, or by any
means, without prior permission in writing from the publisher.

Typeset in Avenir by Marie Doherty

Printed and bound in the UK by Clays Ltd, St Ives plc

About the author

Patricia Furness-Smith is a psychologist and accredited practitioner with 25 years of experience in clinical practice. She has lectured and trained in psychology, psychotherapy and psychopathology for a wide variety of institutions. She is a Fellow of the Chartered Institution of Educational Assessors (CIEA), a Fellow of the Institute for Learning (IfL) and a Fellow of the National Counselling Society (NCS). In addition, she is a member of the British Association for the Person-Centred Approach (BAPCA) and the British Association for Counselling and Psychotherapy (BACP).

As well as running her own private practice, she is a clinical supervisor, moderator, examiner, reviewer, validator, magistrate, freelance writer and consultant on British Airways' 'Flying with Confidence' courses. She is the co-author of *Flying with Confidence: The Proven Programme to Fix your Flying Fears* and sole author of the guided relaxation CD of the same title. Her particular specialisms are in relationships, eating disorders and phobias. She has recently published *Introducing Overcoming Phobias: A Practical Guide* and *Introducing Overcoming Problem Eating: A Practical Guide.*

She enjoys an international reputation as a specialist in hodophobia (the fear of travelling). She is often quoted in the media and has appeared in national and foreign newspapers and magazines and on radio, television and social media sites.

Author's note

It's important to note that there is much frequently used research within the various fields under discussion in this book. Where I am able to cite the source I have done so, but my sincere apologies to the originators of any material if I have overlooked them within this book.

Furthermore, in order to respect client privacy and anonymity within the case studies described, I have formed composite characters by scrambling personal details and changing names.

In addition, if you have any medical condition, it is always important to check with your GP whether the various exercises described within this book are appropriate for you.

Dedication

The most beautiful soul I ever met.
Alex Carington

This book is dedicated to Buffy, an individual of such singular inner beauty and loveliness that even the brightest celestial body in our firmament is eclipsed by her sheer brilliance.

May we aspire to follow her example and be ready to live with an open and loyal heart, acknowledging that our greatest treasures are not what we possess but our loving relationships with one another, be they family, friends or even strangers.

Let us be willing to be moved by the simple things in life, such as the foolish antics of a puppy chasing its tail, sitting with dear friends around a campfire or relishing the smell of newly baked chocolate croissants, just begging to be eaten.

If we can imbibe her innate wisdom by truly recognizing the meaning of life, that is, embracing every opportunity offered with fearlessness, optimism and humour, we can learn to be vibrantly alive. To Buffy every day was a special day; living in the moment was her trademark.

Begin doing what you want to do now. We are not living in eternity. We have only this moment, sparkling like a star in our hand – and melting like a snowflake.

Sir Francis Bacon

Buffy's example has been a lesson to so many – that the secret of fulfilment and positive well-being is to be steadfastly true to oneself, never sheltering behind guises or needing endorsement from others. This she did with effortless grace, authenticity and integrity – never marching to anyone else's drum, no matter what the consequences.

In short, Buffy comprehended the meaning of contentment by being grateful for both the minutiae and the epic moments of life. Her inimitable brand of obstinate optimism put even Pollyanna in the shade. No smile, laughter, friend, challenge or experience was wasted upon her. To Buffy, life was a big adventure, which she sprinted out to meet, embracing it with arms wide open. As William Wallace so poignantly and tragically observed: 'Every man dies, not every man really lives.' This charge could never be levied at Buffy, who from a tender age had mastered the art of living. I stand in awe of her insight, loveliness and energy and am totally humbled and grateful for all the love and inspiration she gave so unstintingly.

She walked the talk, which you will find within these pages, and left in her wake a trail of love, joy and happiness. She also personified the expression 'a sight for sore eyes', since just a glimpse of her infectious smile made even the most dispirited and disaffected among us feel restored, invigorated and hopeful.

Buffy's favourite saying and the code by which she lived was:

It's not the years in your life that count but the life in your years.

How utterly privileged I am, that you are my daughter.

Contents

Preface   1

PART ONE: Understanding well-being   **7**
1. What is well-being?   9
2. Eudaemonic and hedonic well-being   17
3. The person-centred approach (PCA)   25
4. Human givens approach (HGA)   39
5. The nervous system and vagus nerve   47

PART TWO: Wakefulness and well-being   **65**
6. Building a healthy approach to life   67
7. Exercise and fitness   91
8. Eating well   101
9. Relaxation   117

PART THREE: Well-being and sleep   **141**
10. What is sleep and why do we do it?   143
11. Practical advice to improve sleep   157
12. Sleep problems and treatments   175
13. Insomnia   183

Final word   199
Useful contacts   203
Acknowledgements   209
Index   211

Preface

*We live longer than our forefathers, but we suffer more from
a thousand artificial anxieties and cares. They fatigued only
the muscles; we exhaust the finer strength of the nerves.*

Edward George Bulwer-Lytton

For the past 25 years I have worked with numerous clients who have suffered from a wide range of issues, which have caused them untold distress. My experience has taught me that regardless of the affliction, for example depression or alcoholism, the *disease*, *dys*function, *dis*sonance, *dis*connection – call it what you will – is merely a manifestation of something that is not working within their life, resulting in a sense of negative well-being. So I am delighted to be writing this book, which provides the antidote to becoming a candidate for such suffering. It is a little known fact that your sense of well-being is largely in your *own* hands. This book will help you not only to recognize this reality but will also provide you with the necessary tools to maximize your potential, enabling you to achieve positive well-being, a vital component of a contented and fulfilled life.

So if you wish to augment your state of positive well-being, improve your physical health and increase your resilience to falling prey to mental illness, then this is the book for you. Few of us have been left unscathed by the impact of poor physical or mental health, be it via personal experience or knowing someone close to us who has suffered from either, or both, of these types of health concerns.

Today we have seen a tremendous escalation in both mental and physical ill health throughout world populations. The higher incidence in mental health disorders is partly attributable to greater public awareness, which has encouraged people to come forward to seek help for their anxiety or depression rather than suffering in silence.

However, there is no doubt that mental ill health is afflicting increasingly younger people, whether it be manifested through addictions, eating disorders, obsessive compulsive disorder or phobias, to mention but a few of the many ways people experience mental illnesses. At the other end of the spectrum there is clear evidence that dementia and depression are becoming more widespread, and this is not entirely down to the fact that people are living longer.

Equally, despite huge advances in medical knowledge, major physical illnesses (such as cancers, heart disease and diabetes) continue to proliferate, be they caused by pollution, eating habits, alcohol abuse, too much stress, inadequate sleep or something else. We can no longer be blind to 'the writing on the wall' and must take steps to secure our own positive well-being by being pro-active in this quest.

Perhaps the most sobering indicator of our levels of well-being can be gleaned from the ever-increasing number of suicides and attempted suicides across the globe. To elect to end one's life provides the ultimate barometer of negative well-being in the vast majority of cases. I say that this only applies to the majority and not all people who fall in to this category, since some of the incidences would actually qualify for 'assisted suicide' (or 'self-deliverance') were this option available to them. By this I am referring to those who make a conscious, measured decision to end their life since they do not wish to suffer the indignity and pain of a degenerative disease, for example.

Suicide in many countries was previously partially held in check because it had been seen as a criminal act, which would have an impact on both suicide attempt survivors and the families of those who had been successful. Also secularization has dented the influence of the church and its religious condemnation (and consequent stigmatization) of such acts.

As a marker of dissatisfaction with life, we can see its close link with diminishing levels of positive well-being. However, disconcerting statistics on suicide provide us with clues to the essential ingredients required for positive well-being: namely the sense of having control over our existence, belonging and connectivity with others via family and friendship networks; the opportunity to contribute meaningfully towards life; and the ability to fulfil our dreams and potential. Nobody sails through life without problems and difficulties, but we can certainly learn how to mitigate the damage and not only survive but live our lives to the full. In this book I will show you how.

How is the book organized?

The book is divided into three sections. The first part discusses why we should address our level of positive well-being and the other two parts explain how to achieve this goal. I recommend that part 1 is read first since this will explain to you the incredible power you possess in being able to influence your own and others' positive well-being. The other two parts and their individual chapters can be dipped in to in any order of preference, depending upon your area of interest.

Part 1 explores the meaning of well-being and the various influences which have an effect on well-being. It also briefly considers two psychological approaches, which I have found very useful in establishing positive well-being on a firm footing within my client work. I then discuss important aspects of our own biology, which enable us to increase our positive well-being by looking at the role played by our nervous system.

Part 2 consists of tips, techniques and practical exercises that can be used to improve our positive well-being during what takes up roughly two thirds of our life, that is, the time that we are awake. This covers topics such as eating, exercising, relaxation and attitudes.

Part 3 considers the importance of the remaining third of our life, which ideally is spent sleeping. I have dedicated an entire section to sleep, since if we manage to get this notional eight hours of our day right, it will largely dictate how successfully we can manage the other sixteen hours.

Who is this book for?

This book is intended for a wide readership, encompassing all those who have suffered from negative well-being across the spectrum to those who wish to continue to enjoy their current levels of positive well-being, as 'prevention is better than cure'. In short, every one of us can benefit from consciously considering the many factors that play their part in enabling us to live our lives to the full.

The ancient founder of philosophical Taoism was ahead of the game in knowing the vital ingredients of positive well-being. It is sobering to recognize how far we have strayed over the past two-and-a-half millennia from this utterly inspirational advice as we hustle and bustle through our everyday lives.

In dwelling, live close to the ground.
In thinking, keep to the simple.
In conflict, be fair and generous.
In governing, don't try to control.
In work, do what you enjoy.
In family life, be completely present.
Lao Tzu

PART ONE:
Understanding well-being

1. What is well-being?

What do we mean by well-being?

The phrase, 'state of well-being' is often bandied about, but what do we actually mean by this expression? It is a rather nebulous phrase, which many interpret as synonymous with welfare or level of happiness, state of physical or mental health or degree of satisfaction with life.

Perhaps the above factors do form part of what we mean by this term, but not necessarily so. For example, let us speculate upon Andrea Bocelli, the renowned Italian tenor who became blind at the age of twelve. Must his level of positive well-being be significantly compromised as a consequence of his physical infirmity? There is every possibility that Bocelli might enjoy a very high level of positive well-being despite his lack of sight, since estimation of one's well-being is a highly subjective phenomenon.

As the author Antoine de Saint-Exupéry perspicaciously implies in a 1943 story entitled, *Le Petit Prince*, it is what we think of ourselves that counts and determines our state of well-being. However, what we think of ourselves, for good or ill, can be greatly influenced by what others think of us:

> *I have no right, by anything I do or say, to demean*
> *a human being in his own eyes. What matters is not*
> *what I think of him; it is what he thinks of himself.*

Objective measures of well-being

Yes, we can attempt to measure welfare or well-being in accordance with objective measures, such as where a person may be located on various scales (be they economic, social, psychological, physical or even spiritual), but none of these actually captures the reality of well-being as experienced by the individual.

In my practice I have met many people who ostensibly have no business not to enjoy high levels of positive well-being, having wealth, status, good health, loving relationships, interesting careers and so much more. And yet, these individuals come to me suffering from depression, anger, addictions, eating disorders and anxiety, to name but a few of the mental health afflictions which I treat. Clearly, objective measures alone do not provide an accurate assessment for an individual's state of well-being.

Positive well-being is about meeting our expectations

It is abundantly obvious that being adequately fed, watered, housed and exercised, along with being gainfully employed and well-educated and enjoying excellent physical health, are all components that facilitate positive well-being, but they are far from the whole story.

Well-being is primarily concerned with the degree to which our expectations, dreams and aspirations are met, and these are totally unique to each individual. Many of our attitudes are a direct result of our 'nurturing' and this, along with our own aptitudes and personality – our 'nature' – mingle together to form ideals of what success looks like for each of us.

Culture influences our sense of well-being

Depending upon our cultural heritage we might favour a collective or individualistic approach to life (or maybe a combination of the two), and this will colour our estimation of personal well-being. In a strictly collectivist society, blending into the group and not drawing attention to oneself generates feelings of acceptance, belonging and comfort. Even if the price paid is conceding to a high degree of conformity to group expectations, this will still work towards affording a sense of positive well-being for the majority who have been socialized in this manner. (The subjective experience of well-being is explained further in chapter 2; see p. 22.)

We are not all equally malleable in conforming to society's conventions

However, there are mavericks in every society, where the personal imperative outstrips that of the social; these highly autonomous individuals buck the trend and follow their own course of action, often at their peril. Not to follow their own star would lead to considerable inner conflict and result in a state of negative well-being. Many of this ilk find themselves 'damned if they do and damned if they don't' in subscribing to normative behaviour.

These people, by not conforming, invite society's disapproval or, by conceding to society's expectations, they feel that they have not been true to themselves and experience dissonance. Dissonance is a state of mental conflict when you experience contradictory emotions and beliefs. In the not-too-distant past, working women who wished to pursue their career after having children faced this dilemma. Similarly, the converse was true for stay-at-home fathers who flouted society's expectation that the male should be the chief breadwinner.

Society's sanctions

A more up-to-date example are the brave men and women in the public arena who openly state their homosexuality. Openly gay politicians and sports personalities are a relatively recent phenomenon. Unfortunately, there are still some countries in which homosexuality is considered a criminal offence. To openly express anything other than a heterosexual disposition runs the risk of penalties such as imprisonment or even death. This can engender severe negative well-being for those who have to suppress an intrinsic part of their personal identity.

Think of a situation where you have been part of a group and acquiesced to comments or behaviour of which you disapproved and then bitterly resented the fact that you didn't have the courage to speak up and express your true view. How did this impact your state of well-being?

Conversely, think of a situation where you did speak out and experienced the group's censure and condemnation. How did this impact your state of well-being?

Individualistic society

In fiercely individualistic societies, being indistinguishable from the pack tends to promote negative well-being, since leadership, power and talent differentiate an individual from the herd, attracting kudos and admiration. Individualistic socialization demands that we stand out from the crowd if we are to feel good about ourselves and enjoy enhanced positive well-being. This pressure can be seen in cultures that emphasize educational attainment, and prestigious institutions can foster individualism to even higher degrees, if you pardon the pun.

Collectivist versus individualistic

The powerful impact of nurturing and socialization, resulting in the inculcation of society's expectations, mores and values can be seen in the contrast between collectivist and individualistic societies. Public shame has a far greater negative impact on well-being in Japan, a collectivist society, than it has in contemporary Europe, which favours a more individualistic approach. One only has to look at the number of disgraced European bankers or politicians who have bounced back into public life, subsequent to their humiliation and ruination. In contrast, a number of Japanese prime ministers and business leaders have accepted personal responsibility for their government's or organization's shortcomings in the last decade, often resigning their positions. Today, in European society, people tolerate a variety of responses. Some applaud the manifestations of honour and integrity which resignation signals, while others praise the resilience of those who insist upon remaining in post.

The important thing to keep in mind is that societal attitudes are constantly changing and evolving, yet many people can get stuck in a time warp and hold on to childhood perceptions about themselves and feelings, such as shame, which negatively impact their well-being. It is advisable to constantly reassess your perceptions of experience and work out if the view you are holding is in line with your current values and beliefs. Often when you go through this process you will recognize that you are carrying parental, peer or societal attitudes that are not in tune with your own moral compass, and which therefore need to be updated.

In my role as a trainer, I frequently encounter people who have little belief in their academic ability, based on negative experiences that happened when they were young. For example, educators today are far more enlightened and recognize dyslexia as a condition that in no way reflects a lack of academic ability. Similarly, today's children who are left-handed are no longer compelled to go against their natural disposition and forced to learn to write with their right hand, which in the past hindered both their development and confidence levels. There are numerous examples of the fluidity of societal attitudes in recent years with regard to illegitimacy, regional accents, ageing and bisexuality, to name but a few; however people frequently fail to update their inner tapes acquired from childhood.

THINK ABOUT IT

Remember that unchallenged historical perceptions become carved in stone and can have a detrimental impact on your well-being. What unfounded limiting beliefs are you currently holding on to, which if revised would enable you to find greater fulfilment?

---

2. Eudaemonic and hedonic well-being

An important component which feeds into our level of well-being is the way in which the prevailing culture emphasizes the importance of hedonism or eudaemonism. Hedonism is the lifestyle we associate with the Epicureans or modern stockbrokers, whereas eudaemonism is favoured by the Quakers and philanthropists. Looking at these terms in a very simplistic way, we associate hedonism with behaviours such as indulging in lavish meals or shopping sprees and eudaemonism with championing worthy causes and performing 'good works'. Of course, ranges of possibilities lie in between these two purist positions, and most developed societies advocate a combination of the two, encapsulated in the saying 'all work and no play makes Jack a dull boy'. This, of course, ties in with the discussion in chapter 1 about meeting the expectations of society.

KEY TERMS

Eudaemonic well-being is derived from the feelings of satisfaction that we enjoy as a result of being able to *contribute* in a meaningful way in life. This endows us with a sense of usefulness and purpose. It is often achieved through 'transcendence', whereby we virtuously devote ourselves to others or a cause, rather than focusing on our own immediate desires and sensual pleasures.

Hedonic well-being is often seen as a more self-centred route to well-being, in which we indulge in pursuits that give us personal satisfaction. 'Hedonist' can be a pejorative term denoting a character who is consumed with the desire to indulge bodily pleasures to excess. *yes*

It may appear that one form of well-being is intrinsically selfish while the other is inherently altruistic, but this is not the case. My own view is that both avenues are important to achieving an overall positive sense of well-being. Humans are complex creatures and positive well-being is derived from embracing our entire being in all its superficiality and depth.

THINK ABOUT IT Try to identify when you feel good about yourself. What activity are you engaged in when you feel good about yourself, and what other emotions do you experience? What is the combination of hedonic and eudaemonic fulfilment that suits you best? Depending on your disposition and cultural heritage, too much of one or the other can elicit either guilt or joylessness. If you do feel guilty or unhappy about yourself, seek out a balance of eudaemonic and hedonic experiences that suit your natural disposition and expectations to achieve maximum positive well-being.

Combined route to positive well-being

Holidays and sensory treats, such as consuming a delicious meal or smoking a fine cigar (hedonic fulfilment), tend to be more enjoyable when we feel that we deserve these pleasures. By virtue of our achievements through hard work within a meaningful career (eudaemonic fulfilment), we earn the right to spoil ourselves from time to time and feel justified in doing so. Thus, we can see that for some people a mixture of hedonic and eudaemonic behaviours can blend perfectly to create positive well-being. Other people have a naturally more altruistic nature or have been socialized to place more emphasis on altruism. We could hypothesize that the child of a vicar might be brought up to place more emphasis on eudaemonic fulfilment whereas a pop star's child might be exposed to a more hedonistic lifestyle. So, like everything else in life, the blend of nature and nurture is unique to each individual, and we can only apply generalizations to populations. If we look at prominent individuals we can readily identify that North Korea's supreme leader Kim Jong-un and former South African president Nelson Mandela demonstrated quite polarized positions rather than a blended approach.

During the Second World War, against a backdrop of intense uncertainty about the future, both hedonistic and eudaemonic behaviour became culturally endorsed in the West. Many survivors of the war claimed that it was a time in their life that they felt exquisitely alive. Since each day might have been their last, they lived intensely in the moment. Hedonic happiness was literally snatched from the jaws of death, leading to an escalation of sexually permissive behaviour, drinking and smoking. At the same time, eudaemonic behaviour also peaked. Individuals gained a sense of meaning and purpose and, in turn, positive well-being by fighting for their country and freedom.

THINK ABOUT IT We can appreciate the merit in the old maxim, 'a little of what you fancy does you good'. Indeed, in my work as a psychologist I frequently encourage my clients who are trying to effect change to reward themselves with a little treat as they reach each milestone, as a way of reinforcing the new behaviour. Parents do this automatically and reward their children's achievements with, for example, trips to the zoo, since hedonic pleasures clearly boost happiness, self-esteem and other building blocks of positive well-being, motivating the child to aspire even further.

You can have too much of a good thing

It is not unheard of that people who have won the lottery and have been catapulted into hedonistic pursuits become depressed. A lifetime of finding meaning and purpose through work – either by achieving *intrinsic* satisfaction (having an interesting and challenging career) or *extrinsic* satisfaction (work being a means of providing for one's family) – can vanish overnight.

As a consequence, eudaemonic well-being may plummet and the individual might well find the surfeit of hedonistic pastimes a poor substitute that does not sit well with the value system which they previously embraced. For this reason, many people in this situation give substantial amounts of their financial windfall to charities and retain much of their former lifestyle.

CASE STUDY Poverty may not necessarily cause negative well-being. Our attitudes can determine our degree of positive or negative well-being; thus it is possible for the poorest person to feel much higher levels of positive well-being than someone who seems to have it all but experiences discontent. Mother Teresa, a Catholic nun and missionary who received the Nobel Peace Prize for her charitable work, clearly thrived upon the eudaemonic route to positive well-being, finding fulfilment through her work with the poor and infirm. In contrast, Imelda Marcos, the politician and former first lady of the Philippines who was once exiled for fraud, pursued the hedonic variety – finding happiness and satisfaction in the acquisition of enormous wealth and the collection of material possessions, such as shoes.

Were each of these women to have been offered the other's lifestyle, it is conceivable that both would have suffered states of considerable negative well-being: Mother Theresa experiencing acute guilt as a result of the extravagance and excess and Marcos suffering a sense of privation due to the paucity of personal possessions and wealth.

Bringing our potential to fruition

Positive well-being is therefore the *sense* of fulfilment: the experience of believing that we are able to achieve through life that which is meaningful to us. The extent to which we subjectively feel that we are flourishing or moving towards meeting our potential is the key determinant of our well-being and this, thankfully, is not entirely dependent upon external circumstances and society's expectations.

Well-being is an elusive, somewhat ethereal quality, which can only be evaluated by individuals for themselves. To some individuals, their sense of flourishing may lie in their ability to acquire wealth, power, status or material possessions. To others, discovery, invention, diplomacy, creativity or philanthropy may be key. The aristocratic French writer Antoine de Saint-Exupery stated: 'You can only see properly with your heart. The essential is invisible to the eye.' So it is the case with one's sense of well-being: it is a subjective valuing of our visceral experience of life.

 It is possible for the most selfish character to enjoy positive well-being in the same way that the kindest and most generous soul may endure negative well-being. This may not seem fair, but then it is irrational to assume that life should be fair. Anyone reading this book has clearly been endowed with a significant resource: the opportunity to learn to read. Great swathes of the world's population can only dream about the chance of receiving an education. Do you feel blessed because of this, or do you compare yourself to some of your contemporaries instead and regard yourself as less fortunate?

We can proactively enhance positive well-being

Natural forces within us are the true healers of disease.

Hippocrates

Many health professionals now accept that the patient can play an active part in the maintenance and recovery of both well-being and physical wellness, regardless of age, wealth, health or a multitude of other factors. In the next chapters you will learn how to increase positive emotions and good physical health while limiting your vulnerability to falling prey to illness. We all have it in our gift to promote positive well-being in both others and ourselves by adopting some simple daily routines and practices; indeed the best things in life are free, such as breathing correctly, taking exercise and sleeping well. All we have to do is discipline ourselves to embrace them.

3. The person-centred approach (PCA)

Seek out that particular mental attitude which makes you feel most deeply and vitally alive, along with which comes the inner voice which says, 'This is the real me,' and when you have found that attitude, follow it.

William James

William James beautifully encapsulates the essence of a talking therapy known as the *person-centred approach* (PCA). This psychological theory, or 'way of being', was developed and advocated by Carl Rogers, a humanistic psychologist in the last century. I find this form of therapy enormously helpful in facilitating positive well-being in my clients. PCA places great importance upon personal authenticity and genuineness, what in layman's terms, we often refer to as 'being comfortable in one's own skin'.

Living harmoniously

It is a simple fact of life that when we live in accordance with our beliefs, aptitudes and values we are far happier than when we follow a path that goes against the grain. Rogers, through his own life experience, recognized that when he listened to his inner voice, rather than conforming to the expectations of others, he generally made choices and decisions that proved to be right for him.

He then extrapolated his experience as having universal application. He believed that people fall prey to negative well-being when they become divorced from their true essence in order to win favour and acceptance from significant others. Rogers referred to the 'true self' as the 'organismic self' and the 'ideal self' as the person we think we should be. The greater the gulf between these two selves, the more 'incongruent', or psychologically out of sorts, we will feel.

The **organismic self** is your real self, responsible for sending you trustworthy internal messages, which if heeded keep you in a state of 'congruence', or self-honesty. It will let you know what you need to do to achieve your potential.

The **ideal self** refers to the self which seeks to gain the approval of significant others by adopting their attitudes and ideas of how you should be. The more divorced you become from your organismic self in an attempt to meet other people's expectations, the more psychologically fragile you will become, since you are not being true to yourself.

Positive regard and conditions of worth

Rogers referred to the search for love and approval as the need for 'positive regard' from others, which is contingent upon complying with other people's *conditions of worth* (COW). COW are not to be confused with the necessary guidance and feedback from others that we all need throughout our life. A condition of worth is negative because it makes an individual only feel valued and accepted when they conform to another's rules or conditions. It tends to focus on an individual's behaviour and to deny their intrinsic worth as a human being and thus becomes a form of control, whether done consciously or unconsciously. A simple example of a condition of worth is a parent letting a child know that they will only be acceptable if they are well mannered and share their toys with their friends. The child, wishing to court their parent's approval and believing that love is conditional upon them behaving themself will try to show how generous and considerate they are towards their friend. They will carry out this cooperative behaviour even though secretly it pains them to let the other child handle their favourite doll or train set.

To resist conditions of worth can be overwhelmingly difficult, and one just has to think about the rejection and treatment meted out to conscientious objectors during the First and Second World Wars to appreciate the compulsion to conform. The powerful condition of worth 'that it is sweet and right to die for your country' was immortalized in the famous war poet Wilfred Owen's words. Fortunately, many societies, particularly in the West, now recognize that people are entitled to freedom of thought and expression, and there is greater acceptance of diversity.

If people are not encumbered by other people's expectations or COW, they will be enabled to move continually

towards meeting their potential. The analogy that garden-
ers do not grow flowers since flowers grow themselves is
very apposite when describing this approach. In the same
way that a good gardener will endeavour to provide the
best environment in which the flowers can thrive, a person-
centred therapist strives to provide the best conditions for
the client to grow and flourish, confident in the belief that
the client has within themself all that is needed to fulfil their
potential.

Once you understand that you are the best judge of
what is right for you, you will start to listen to your inner
voice. Each of us is unique and, as Rogers stated, it is only
the individual who knows what hurts or provides them with
pleasure. For example, would you dream of deferring to
someone else's opinion as to what type of meal you enjoy
the most? This is clearly ludicrous, and yet many of us defer
to others on fundamental issues such as whom we should
marry or what career we should choose. If we have serious
doubts as to whether something feels right for us, then in all
likelihood it is not. The sensible parent, partner and friend
will always encourage you to follow your own instinct on
such matters.

 Next time you have a decision to make, try to
provide yourself with the most favourable conditions in which you can make this decision.

1. Be honest with yourself and really listen to how you feel about the matter.

2. Be non-judgemental and recognize that your opinion is the most important of all.

3. Ensure that you have the best information available upon which to base your decision. Seek counsel from others, but ultimately the decision must be yours.

4. Evaluate the pros and cons related to your options and choose the option that fits most closely to your values, principles and personal goals.

Covert conditions of worth

When selecting my O-Level classes, I injudiciously chose physics over art, which I adored. This choice was as a result of having a chartered nuclear engineer for a father and my erroneous deduction that sciences would be held in greater esteem than the arts. Although I had been given a totally free choice of subject selection, with no overt direction, I instinctively thought that I would gain more approval by choosing physics.

As it turned out, this choice was a big mistake, since velocity, acceleration and the like did nothing for me. It was not until many years later that I heard my parents say it was such a shame that I did not pursue art, since they thought it a wonderful thing to be able to do!

Our *perception* is what really matters. Conditions of worth can be misinterpreted.

Organismic valuing process

The child sharing their toys is an innocuous example as it socializes them to mix effectively with other children. However, many other COW can be downright harmful, such as telling a child it is wrong to disagree, show anger or express emotion. Maxims such as 'big boys don't cry', 'children should be seen and not heard' and 'keep a stiff upper lip' send powerful messages that teach us to distrust our emotions and comply with what others expect of us. From early childhood we learn to override our natural tendencies in favour of the preferences and predilections of significant others, be they parents, teachers, peers or even partners.

Happily, things are changing, and the 1950s COW for women in the West to be demure, domesticated and obedient to their husbands' guidance would now get short shrift from most women. Yet, an ambitious woman today is often still described as 'shrill' or 'bossy', descriptors that would not be applied to a man in a similar role. Equally, not all men wish to be captains of industry or aspire to macho behaviour, a pressure that many men face. Those wishing to follow different paths must resist some pretty compelling societal COW.

The suppression of our own inner counsel in favour of others' expectations was referred to by Rogers as losing touch with our 'organismic valuing process', our internal mechanism that tells us what feels right or wrong. When we disregard our inner voice we usually experience discomfort, disappointment and even guilt. These discordant emotions derail us from our path towards positive well-being and can foster states of anxiety, depression and low self-esteem.

THINK ABOUT IT Can you recall a time, as a teenager, when you went against your instinct or principles in order to gain the approval of your peers? Maybe it was that first cigarette or alcoholic drink, which you did not actually enjoy but which you felt you could not refuse without being excluded from the group. Or perhaps you can recall telling a lie or not owning up to something you did and allowing another to take the blame. How did it make you feel?

Congruence
By promoting a phenomenological approach, that is respecting the unique subjective experience of individuals, Rogers was able to facilitate his clients to achieve higher degrees of harmony in their lives. This he termed as living in a state of congruence.

KEY TERMS

A **phenomenological approach** looks at how an individual constructs their perception of reality as a result of the subjective interpretations they draw from experience. Objective phenomena, such as aircraft turbulence, will be interpreted differently by each individual. To a passenger, turbulence can be interpreted as dangerous, whereas to a pilot, it is merely inconvenient, since it may delay the meal service.

Congruence refers to the consistency between a person's self-perception and their experience. If a boy cries because he has fallen and hurt himself, this is congruent behaviour. If an adult then tells him that big boys don't cry, he will experience confusion and **incongruence**, wanting to please the adult on the one hand but denying his own feelings on the other.

TRY IT NOW!

This exercise will enable you to determine your own level of congruence. A useful starting point is to think back to the family maxims which were around when you were growing up. For example, perhaps you were urged always to clear your plate and now feel guilty if you do not eat everything put in front of you.

1. Make a list of the conditions of worth you grew up with.

2. Make a second list of any conditions of worth you have

acquired in your adult life from friends, a partner or colleagues.

3. Take stock of the two lists and decide if there are any conditions that are holding you back from being your 'true self' or achieving your dreams.

4. If there is anything that doesn't fit with who you feel you are, decide how you are going to liberate yourself by jettisoning that COW from your life.

Having completed this exercise you may feel that you would benefit further from the support of a person-centred therapist; you will find information on this approach in the Useful contacts section towards the end of the book.

How does the PCA work?

Rogers believed that by offering a client a special environment in which they could explore their issues, the client would be able to find solutions to their problems or acceptance of their situation. This environment required six conditions, all of which he believed were both necessary and sufficient to facilitate therapeutic change in the client. They basically boil down to a relationship in which the client, who is seeking help to resolve their difficulties, experiences their practitioner as 'congruent', or genuine, non-judgemental and empathic.

By the therapist offering total acceptance, known as 'unconditional positive regard', the client no longer needs to defend, justify or suppress their feelings. The practitioner has no expectations of their client and in this atmosphere of total freedom the conditions of worth can be dissolved and the client can reconnect with their organismic self.

These six conditions can be fostered in everyday life by each and every one of us to provide the most conducive environment for healthy relationships. However, it is not quite so straightforward to achieve the high levels of the core conditions to which a therapist aspires because we will have a vested interest in the relationship for our own needs to be met too, which is not the case for the practitioner who is not personally affected by the client's choices and behaviours.

The importance of unconditional positive regard
If you are a parent, do you ever say to your child: 'I am so proud of you for winning that race (or coming top in an exam)'? If you do say things of this nature, I strongly urge you to stop, because your child will learn to try to win your love and approval through success. When the child fails or does not do so well, they will equate this with a diminishment of your love, acceptance and approval. You and I are adults and know that this is not the case and that you love your child unconditionally, but that is not the message that you are sending, and this is where the damage starts.

This experience of conditional approval, respect or love is not limited to just the parent-child relationship but is endemic in all other relationships and can be equally destructive. Comments to your romantic partner that you are proud of them when they achieve a promotion or to your employee that you really value them for securing the highest sales figures in the company send a similar message, which is that you only recognize and show affection to them when they are successful.

With your child, try saying something along the lines of: 'You must be so thrilled or proud of what you have achieved by practising so much or studying so hard.' This way the child learns to do things for their own satisfaction and achievement and, most importantly, knows that they are always a winner in your eyes no matter what the outcome. I have worked with a number of siblings of talented children who have grown up in their shadow and have developed inferiority complexes. It is very rare for a parent to say 'bravo, I am so proud of you for coming last', but the less gifted child feels the dearth of praise in comparison to their sibling's constant recognition.

The greatest gift you can give your child, friend, employee or lover is self-confidence, and this starts by building their sense of empowerment, autonomy and self-esteem based upon themself, rather than thinking that they are only worthy if you can bask in the reflected glory of their success. It is needless to say that children in particular are highly impressionable; so if you are a teacher, scout master, youth leader or play any role in working with children, take this on board too.

Children should not be raised as performing seals and it is only through inculcating values of personal self-respect that they will become self-policing adults with integrity, taking responsibility for their own destiny. Everyone deserves the right to enjoy their own uniqueness and not be compared with others. After all, we each have entirely different talents and resources, so pitting one against the other is futile, nonsensical and damaging. It is far more intelligent to encourage a person to judge themself against themself as this is the only fair comparison.

In fact this guidance permeates all relationships, since we all want to be valued for our own sake. It often comes as a surprise to adult children to recognize that their parents need unconditional love too, particularly in their old age when the opportunity to achieve and impress can be seriously diminished through illness and infirmity. In my work I have often observed individuals blossoming as a result of extricating themselves from controlling relationships for a new partnership in which they are free to be true to themselves. To know that you are loved just because you are *you* is an intoxicating confidence booster.

So many adults constantly crave acknowledgements and endorsements from others; they do not know how to self-soothe since they can only see their value through another's approval. Many celebrities are decimated by a poor review having learnt to be needy for acclaim and adoration. In the end it is only the individual who can judge if they have lived their life well. Andre Agassi, an extraordinarily successful former tennis player who held the world number one ranking in the 1990s, is a salutary example of how we can go completely against our true nature and get caught up in the need to gain approval from significant others. Agassi detested playing professional tennis because of the pressure, but did not want to disappoint his family.

When it comes to dishing out conditions of worth – don't do it to others and don't allow it to be done to yourself.

Summary

By exploring the person-centred approach, we can appreciate how the seeds of negative well-being are sewn from a tender age as a result of conditions of worth, which can exert their influence throughout a person's life. When clients present for therapy the practitioner will facilitate the stripping away of these encumbrances, which will enable the individual to reconnect with their true nature.

Although this approach looks disarmingly simple, it takes considerable self-development for the practitioner to truly offer what are known as the 'core conditions' of empathy, unconditional positive regard and congruence. Practitioners, like their clients, are works of art in progress and continually strive to nurture and improve their ability to offer these conditions. In choosing to foster this approach yourself, you will not only enable improvements to your relationships with others but, more importantly, you will move towards achieving self-acceptance, a crucial component of positive well-being. Self-acceptance can be elusive when you try to be what others want you to be by following in their footsteps rather than forging your own path. After all, as the minister and popular author John Mason points out: 'You're born an original. Don't die a copy.'

4. Human givens approach (HGA)

The *human givens approach* (HGA) provides excellent psychological scaffolding on which to build sound positive well-being. Although a relative newcomer to the wide range of talking therapies on offer, the HGA has ancient antecedents.

This approach garners useful aspects of existing therapies derived from antiquity onwards and roots its applied techniques in the latest neuroscience, thus producing a highly pragmatic, expedient and efficient model of therapy.

Emotional needs and resources to meet these needs

This set of 'organizing ideas', drawn from existing therapies, was formally compiled by Joe Griffin and Ivan Tyrrell in the late 20th century and called 'human givens'. This approach operates from the stance that we all have basic *emotional needs*, which need to be met to ensure good health and well-being. The second key premise is that nature has endowed us with the *necessary resources* to get these essential needs met, either from within ourselves or from our environment.

These needs are basic common sense, but it is surprising how often we ignore the obvious. This chapter will enable you to check whether all of your emotional needs are being met. If any are not being sufficiently fulfilled, you will be able to focus on this need to remedy the situation to enhance your positive well-being. You can do this for yourself by using your own innate resources or you can seek the support and guidance of a human givens therapist if you prefer.

Human givens is a term for both our emotional needs and our resources to supply these needs.

It has long been accepted that humans have basic *physical* needs, such as the requirement for unpolluted air to breathe, uncontaminated water to drink and essential nutrients to eat in order to survive. Increasingly we are recognizing the significance of basic *emotional* needs being met to ensure sound mental and physical health.

Emotional needs

You might be wondering what our basic emotional needs are. These can be summarized as the need to:

1. Feel safe

2. Be noticed and give attention to others

3. Feel appreciated or enjoy a sense of status

4. Act with a degree of autonomy over the direction of our lives

5. Belong or be accepted by the community

6. Have a close relationship or friendship with at least one other person

7. Experience relevance or purpose to our existence

8. Have sufficient privacy to reflect and make sense of life's experiences

9. Feel a sense of achievement and progression through our efforts

10. Have an emotional rapport with others.

It is essential that all of the needs above are being met to a certain degree. Any need that is not being met sufficiently is likely to be a key stress factor in your life.

Resources to meet these needs

We can meet these needs by using the gifts with which nature has endowed us. These resources are the ability to:

1. Acquire skills, such as language and knowledge of the world, which we can store and retrieve from our memory.

2. Use our social disposition, such as empathy and communication skills, which enables us to connect with others by building alliances, rapport, friendships and romantic relationships.

3. Imagine new possibilities, which enable us to advance and meet our need for challenge and achievement.

4. Analyze, plan and adapt past experience to enlighten new situations so we can comprehend the world in which we live.

5. Dream, in order to process events which have occurred during the day that we have been unable to resolve, thus allowing us to wake up no longer carrying the weight of the previous day's issues.

6. Reflect upon our behaviour, thoughts and feelings with dispassionate detachment.

This pragmatic and succinct approach enables you or the therapist to pin-point the dysfunctional aspects of your life. Having discovered what is amiss, you can then quickly address the emotional needs not being met.

 Fabian had been retired for two years after an extremely demanding but fulfilling career in the diplomatic service. He sought out therapy because he could not understand why he felt so flat and demotivated. Fabian enjoyed a full social life, had a loving wife and children, and a first grandchild was on the way. With his wide connections abroad, Fabian and his wife Consuelo enjoyed fantastic holidays and also frequently engaged in their joint hobby of sailing. Fabian was mystified as to why he felt so discontented when he had such a wonderful life.

After exploring his emotional needs during the session, it became apparent why. Fabian basically felt stymied since his retirement and needed some sort of project that would stretch him and allow him to experience that feeling of striving and achieving.

Being of a dynamic disposition, within a month he had set up a new project that would make demands on his creative talents. In addition, he and his wife began physical training to enable them to take part in an expedition in the Himalayas. This new sense of adventure and challenge made life exciting and fulfilling for Fabian and, although he still enjoys his golf, sailing and holidays, he has realized that he must always have some sort of pursuit that stretches him mentally and physically in order to feel truly engaged with life.

As we can see from this case, Fabian's emotional need to experience a sense of achievement (need nine) was not being sufficiently met. Each of us has different levels of drive and, having enjoyed a demanding career, Fabian was experiencing 'rust out' in retirement. As a high achiever it was imperative that Fabian should embrace new challenges to feel energized and contented with his life. Having identified what was missing, he was able to use his resources of imagination (resource three) and the ability to acquire new skills (resource one) to address the unmet need.

TRY IT NOW!

Do a quick audit of your levels of satisfaction in life by going through the list of emotional needs. For each of the ten needs listed, give yourself a score between one and seven: one meaning this need is not being met at all and seven indicating that this need is being met to the maximum. Any need for which you score three or less needs attention. If you discover that some of your emotional needs are not being adequately met then think about which resources you can use to address this deficit. For example, if your need for a close friendship (need six) is not being met, then you might join some clubs or activities that will enable you to meet like-minded people; use your ability to build rapport and connection with others (resource two) to meet this need.

How did you get on with this exercise? Remember that the scoring is totally subjective – what matters is your evaluation of what is working or not working for you. Just like with colour sense or pain sensitivity, you are the expert on what you see or feel, and this is what counts. Some people have an intense need for attention or a sense of belonging, whereas others are more solitary and self-sufficient in nature. You may have discovered a number of needs that were being poorly met or perhaps just one that scored very low. It is worth noting, as previously mentioned, that we all have different dispositions. You may find when you assess the audit results that you are experiencing 'burn out'. Although your other needs may be being met very well, your life could be too full of commitments, not allowing you sufficient personal time and space to reflect and make sense of your existence (need eight).

In order to feel at our best, all of our emotional needs have to be attended to. Hoping an issue will go away by ignoring it or by channelling energy into another need is not the solution.

Sometimes we bury our head in the sand because we feel that a problem is insurmountable due to a previous trauma; for example, a painful divorce may make us wary about forging future romantic attachments. If you feel that you need help to address an aspect of your life that is negatively affecting your positive well-being, then you might like to seek out a human givens therapist in your area. A little timely guidance and encouragement can help you to uncover resources that you may have forgotten you had. You will find the website for human givens therapists under Useful contacts towards the back of the book.

5. The nervous system and vagus nerve

I find that with many of my clients, the more that they understand what is happening within their body, the more confident they become in applying relaxation techniques. The ability to down-shift your body into a state of relaxation from a state of high arousal or agitation has enormous benefits. It enables you to access the part of the brain where you make decisions and judgements in a calm and measured manner about the situations in which you find yourself.

When you are under pressure, your body releases stress hormones and initiates short-term emergency survival mode, a heightened state of arousal known as the *fight or flight* (F or F) response, which prepares you to respond to a physical threat. By inducing a state of the optimal relaxation mode, known as *rest and digest* (R & D), long-term survival mode resumes, and the conscious mind is back in the driving seat.

In today's relatively safe world (compared to that of our early ancestors), the majority of us do not face physical threats on a regular basis, but we use our fight or flight response frequently for psychological threats, for which it is not designed and for which it can be totally counterproductive. To get yourself into a heightened state of agitation when negotiating the purchase of a new home or when taking a crucial career exam floods your body with stress hormones, preventing you from thinking clearly and stopping you from making sound decisions or forming cogent arguments. In this chapter you will learn how to prevent becoming disabled by worry and agitation, and techniques to calm yourself down when you do become agitated.

What is the nervous system?

The nervous system is simply the communication and control system of the body; it works by conveying electrochemical messages along a complex network of nerve fibres and neurons throughout the body to and from the brain and spinal cord. Your nervous system is responsible for enabling you to think, move and function by regulating all activities. Depending on which survival mode you are in these activities adjust accordingly. In F or F mode, movement is prioritized. In R & D mode, complex thinking is facilitated. Of course, these are polarized positions; there is every combination in between, and learning to adjust in accordance with your requirements is hugely advantageous. For example, an actor needs a certain amount of adrenaline to produce a peak performance and yet still have sufficient mental capacity to deliver their lines. Too relaxed a mode will make the performance lacklustre and robotic, whereas too much arousal could make the performance appear uncontrolled and frenetic.

In humans the nervous system is made up of two distinct parts: the *central nervous system* (CNS), which consists of the brain and the spinal cord, and the *peripheral nervous system* (PNS), which is made up of nerves that are peripheral to the central nervous system. For our purposes, it is the PNS that is of most interest. Those nerves which branch off from the brain are known as the *cranial nerves* (of which there are twelve pairs). The nerves that branch off from the spinal cord are known as *spinal nerves* (of which there are 31 pairs). The cranial nerves mainly serve the head and neck (apart from the very special tenth cranial nerve, the *vagus*), whereas the spinal nerves accommodate the needs of the rest of the body.

The PNS is further divided into the *somatic nervous system* (SoNS), which is responsible for enabling us to achieve voluntary movement and the *autonomic nervous system* (ANS), which is responsible for regulating involuntary processes, such as digesting food or ensuring that our kidneys or liver are doing their job.

NERVOUS SYSTEM					
Peripheral				Central	
Somatic	Autonomic			Spinal cord	Brain
	Sympathetic	*Para-sympathetic*	*Enteric*		

Importantly, some functions of the ANS can be brought under voluntary control, which is exceptionally useful if we want to slow down our heart rate or reduce our blood pressure, for example. The ANS has three distinct parts, consisting of the *enteric nervous system* (ENS), *sympathetic nervous system* (SNS) and *parasympathetic nervous system* (PSNS). It is the latter two parts that concern us, particularly the PSNS, which is the key to being able to relax (through the interface of this system with the paired vagus nerves, which run from the head through the neck into the abdomen). The SNS causes the state of arousal and regulates your F or F response, which prepares your body for emergencies.

As mentioned, the SNS is designed to help you to survive a physical threat, but it is often activated when we face psychological threats, for which it is highly inappropriate. Constant worry primes the F or F mechanism to go off more readily. The only antidote to resetting this response is by learning how to capitalize on the PSNS by applying various relaxation techniques. The SNS and PSNS act in tandem upon the same organs and glands, but their impact causes opposite effects, not dissimilar to the pedals in your car. Your car's accelerator is like the SNS, activating the state of arousal. The brake is like the PSNS, controlling the state of relaxation. The SNS and the PSNS achieve this by means of different activating chemicals known as neurotransmitters. We will consider how to relax in more detail in chapter 9.

REMEMBER THIS!!!

Allowing yourself to be continually stressed and in a perpetual state of anxiety is very demanding on both your mind and body. Your body reprioritizes its activities and neglects non-essential functions like healing, digesting and growing. Chronic worrying depletes your immune system and makes you less able to deal with whatever was concerning you in the first place. So the simple message is that if you can do something about the problem then do it, and if you can't do anything about it, then accept the situation and stop worrying.

I can hear you saying that this is easier said than done, but the alternative is certainly not in your best interest. If you cannot remedy a difficulty then you must accept it, otherwise your problem becomes a 'problem plus', that is, you still have what originally upset you, *plus* your health and resourcefulness will be significantly compromised from the impact this worry will have on the quality of your sleep. We will look at how to put aside the day's concerns on p. 167.

Differences between PSNS and SNS

	PSNS (RELAXATION) ...	SNS (AROUSAL) ...
... decreases	Metabolic rate	Digestion
	Pulse rate	Saliva production
	Blood pressure	

(continued)

	PSNS (RELAXATION) ...	SNS (AROUSAL) ...
... decreases	Breathing rate	
	Lactic acid level	
	Muscle tension	
	Blood flow to muscles	
	Sweating	
	Anxiety levels	
	Pupil constriction	
... normalizes	Blood glucose	
	Fats	
	Blood clotting	
	Brain (relaxed mode)	
... increases	Digestion	Metabolic rate
	Saliva production	Pulse rate
		Blood pressure
		Lactic acid level
		Breathing rate
		Muscle tension
		Blood flow to muscles
		Sweating
		Anxiety levels
		Pupil dilation
		Blood glucose
		Fats
		Blood clotting
		Alertness

So how does this facilitate positive well-being?

Understanding the great range of differences between the two systems of arousal and relaxation can be a very powerful tool if we can learn how to regulate the systems to our advantage. Despite the SNS and PSNS being autonomic, or outside of conscious control, there are three main ways in which we can consciously manipulate them: through our breathing patterns, muscle tension/release and visualization techniques.

Say, for example, you are feeling apathetic but are about to compete in a race. By increasing your speed of breathing, doing a short warm-up, listening to rousing music, evoking energizing imagery or reciting positive mantras, you will find that you automatically induce a more dominant state of arousal.

Conversely, say you are about to give a presentation at work but have just had an argument with your partner and are in high state of arousal. You need to calm down to give your presentation successfully and convince your colleagues of the feasibility of your proposed project. Slowing down your rate of breathing, using tranquil imagery, repeating positive statements (such as 'I feel calm and in control'), listening to soothing music or relaxing your muscles will help you to simmer down and be able to inspire confidence in your colleagues.

When it comes to producing a peak performance, we can learn how to reach our optimal arousal level before too much or too little excitement causes us to become careless and out of control. It is a very fine balance, and each of us must find our own unique level of stimulation. If you are hyper by nature you will need very little extra stimulus to reach your peak before you are tipped over the top, whereas if you are of a slothful or laid-back disposition you will need a kick-start to get going.

This knowledge gives us the tools to meet challenges by boosting our arousal levels so that we can enjoy the fruits of achievement and success. At the same time it enables us to conserve energy, be creative and feel rested and refreshed by enabling us to operate in an energy-efficient manner when a state of relaxation is appropriate.

The vagus nerve

Recent research into the vagus nerve has yielded some very exciting findings, which have an important impact on our ability to increase our positive well-being. The vagus nerve – that tenth pair of cranial nerves – carries out a multitude of important functions and plays a significant role in both our mental and physical well-being. The extraordinary characteristic of the vagus nerve is that we can manipulate it to a considerable extent by non-surgical means known as *vagal manoeuvres*: simple mental and physical techniques that slow the heart rate.

The vagus nerve is known as a *mixed nerve*, having both sensory and motor properties. This enables it to signal messages to and from the various organs of the body to the brain. Although bi-directional, this nerve is primarily used by the body to inform the brain how it is feeling – 80 per cent of its capacity is used in this way (with only 20 per cent of its capacity being employed by the brain to send messages to the body). It is very special since it is the only pair of cranial nerves that migrate beyond the head and neck.

Emerging from the brain, the pair of vagus nerves travel down the neck, dividing into numerous branches that interface with all the major organs, including the heart, liver and lungs. One of its key roles is to instruct major organs to slow down to enable the rest and digest mode when there is no threat to our survival. The beauty of this nerve is it can enable us to chill out and downshift our metabolism, thus preventing us from becoming victims of psychologically-induced anxiety and panic attacks.

Functions of the vagus nerve

Its functions are numerous and consist of:

1. Reducing blood pressure

2. Protecting against inflammatory diseases

3. Signalling of neurogenesis (the formation of new brain cells)

4. Assisting in insulin resistance

5. Blocking of oxidizing agents, which damage the brain and body

6. Improving our ability to sleep

7. Maintaining optimal energy levels

8. Increasing resistance to anxiety and depression

9. Reducing allergic responses

10. Increasing human growth hormone levels

11. Improving the quality of our memories

12. Increasing our longevity

13. Regulating heart rate

14. Enabling speech, breathing and sweating

15. Facilitating the movement of food through the digestive system.

Vagus nerve stimulation (VNS)

Since the 1990s, vagus nerve stimulation has been used for controlling seizures in people suffering from epilepsy. This is achieved by inserting a small device, known as a vagus nerve stimulator, into the chest of patients. The device acts as a sort of pacemaker, enabling vagal nerve activity to be regulated by sending pulses to the nerve by means of electrodes.

This small device has also been adapted to treat people suffering from eating disorders, particularly bulimia nervosa, by inserting the vagus nerve stimulator just below the clavicle. This re-establishes normal vagal nerve activity which has been disrupted by the binge-purge cycle. The US Federal Drug Administration recommends VNS as a treatment for depression, and researchers are exploring further uses of the technology, including in patients with tinnitus.

Vagal tonality

The vagus nerve plays such a key role in so many aspects of our health that learning how to exploit it provides a fundamental breakthrough in our ability to promote positive well-being. Dr Barbara Fredrickson and Dr Bethany Kok of the University of North Carolina have conducted research into the 'index of vagal nerve tone', or 'vagal tonality', the value of which acts as a type of barometer indicating the level of a person's health. Vagal tonality is measured by monitoring someone's heart rate as they breathe in and out. The differential between these two readings gives the level of tonality. The greater the difference between these figures the higher the vagal tone. High vagal tone correlates with good health. A low differential correlates with ill health and can indicate heart problems.

The power of the mind in promoting vagal vitality

In the same study, Frederickson and Kok asked participants to reflect each evening for nine weeks on how they had connected with others throughout the day. The result of this exercise was an increased feeling of relaxation and improvement in physical health, as indicated by an increase in vagal tonality. This, incidentally, supports evidence for the human givens approach (see chapter 4), which posits we have basic emotional needs – including social connection and the giving and receiving of attention – which must be fulfilled in order to foster stable mental health.

Now comes the really important bit: the research discovered a correlation between high vagal tonality and a more optimistic outlook (see p. 85 for a discussion of optimism). The results suggest that a virtuous cycle of optimism and good physical health can be artificially induced by teaching people how to improve their outlook on life and to accept and show compassion towards themselves and others with daily meditation.

The power of meditation and mindfulness

Those who meditate and practise mindfulness have greater powers of concentration and are more attuned to their emotions and their body's physical signals (see p. 127 for more on meditation and mindfulness). Meditators can acknowledge, experience and express them in healthy ways rather than wasting valuable energy in denial or suppression.

The more years a person has practised meditation, the greater the density of those parts of the brain that enable us to regulate emotion. By daily meditation, the natural loss of brain tissue as we age can be retarded, and possibly even reversed according to the latest findings. This has become even more crucial as our expected lifespan continually increases. In the not-too-distant future, living beyond 100 years will become commonplace, due to medical advances and better diets. This sounds great if we maintain a good quality of life, but it becomes a concern when longevity is accompanied by cognitive decline. Daily meditation, therefore, may play an important role in ensuring a good quality of life in our later years.

As you can imagine, these findings are huge, since we can improve our physical health by using our mind. They also offer scientific evidence for the placebo effect, i.e. being treated with something which has no medical potency whatsoever still results in an improvement in the health of the recipient, purely by virtue of the belief that they are receiving help. This in turn increases their emotional positivity and the improved mental state improves the patient's vagal tonality, which in turn boosts physical health.

 Scientific evidence indicates that a healthy mind induces a healthy body and increases longevity.

The power of the body in promoting vagal tonality

By happy coincidence it is not just the mind that can manipulate the tonality of the vagus nerve; we can also manipulate our body to improve vagal tonality. This is particularly useful for people who have an overactive fight and flight response, which fires off indiscriminately where no physical threat is present. We do this through what are known as 'vagal manoeuvres', which are a range of relaxation exercises. If we are feeling stressed and anxious we can reset our body to relaxation mode by employing the following techniques:

1. Deep abdominal breathing
2. Cold water face immersion
3. Tongue immersion
4. Chanting.

Deep abdominal breathing

The following breathing exercise will enable you to rapidly relax by activating the vagus nerve.

1. Sit or lie in a comfortable position with your hands placed over your stomach (below your belly button) and exhale.

2. Breathe in deeply and slowly through the nose to the count of three or four. Fill up your abdomen so that you can feel your hands being pushed outwards as you inhale.

3. Slowly exhale through the mouth to the count of four or five and notice that your hands will move inwards as your abdomen deflates.

4. Continue to do this for at least five minutes and see if you can train yourself to slow your breathing further by

increasing the count of each breath. It is best to make your exhalation slower than your inhalation since this triggers the vagus nerve to cue relaxation mode, enabling the body to heal, digest and rest.

Once you become adept at breathing in this way on demand, you will no longer need to place your hands in position.

 If you find it difficult to slow down your exhalation, try breathing out through a straw. The fewer the breaths you take per minute, the more relaxed you will feel.

Cold water face immersion

Facial immersion, or the 'dive reflex', has been tested on people after they have engaged in vigorous exercise and has been shown to activate the nervous system to produce an instant calming effect. It can also be beneficial to calm you down in non-exercise situations.

1. Pour very cold water into a bowl or sink.

2. Fill your mouth with saliva and immerse your tongue. If you find it difficult to salivate on demand, then sip some warm water and imagine juicy citrus fruits.

3. Keeping your tongue immersed in the saliva, dunk your face into the cold water so that it covers your face up to the hairline. Remain like this for 30 seconds.

 Another way to stimulate the vagus nerve is to follow step two but replace the cold water with a bag of frozen peas. Take the bag of peas, wrapped in a thin cloth to protect your skin, and place it over your face for 30 seconds. You can also use ice cubes in a plastic bag, but I find that the bag of frozen peas makes better contact by being easier to mould over the face.

Tongue immersion

The dive reflex technique is excellent, but when you don't have a sink or a bag of frozen peas to hand, this technique, although less instant, lends itself to numerous situations, such as when you experience tension in a meeting or are awaiting an appointment with the dentist. When you are stressed you will find that your mouth and throat can feel very dry. This is because digestion is no longer a priority in a threatening situation, and therefore salivation decreases as your body moves from normal long-term survival mode to short-term emergency survival mode. This is a common problem for people who are terrified of public speaking, who literally dry up as a consequence of the sympathetic nervous system being on over drive. The following exercise is a simple and convenient way to remedy the problem.

1. Use imagery to help stimulate the production of saliva. Imagine your favourite food: what it looks, tastes, smells and feels like.

2. Try to un-tense your muscles as you do this since the vagus nerve will relay this relaxed state to the brain, also enabling you to salivate more easily.

3. Bathe your tongue in this well of saliva and the vagus nerve will send further messages to the brain to enter a relaxed state.

REMEMBER THIS!!! The body influences the mind and vice versa. Using your mind (imagining a stimulus) to produce a physical response (increased salivation) will induce a feeling of calm (in the mind), which affects other physical responses (such as sweating or shaking). This sets up a virtuous spiral that can improve your physical health and overall positive well-being.

Chanting 'Om'

The practice of chanting originates from transcendental meditation; the most popular mantra used is the word 'Om' because of the powerful positive impact of this sound in producing a relaxation response. Since your vagus nerve interfaces with the ears, the vibration caused by chanting 'Om' stimulates the auricular branch of the nerve, which then signals to the brain to leave arousal mode.

1. Find a relaxed position and focus on your breathing, ensuring that it is slow, deep and regular.

2. Take a deep breath, and as you exhale, say the 'O' part of 'Om', holding the note for five seconds.

3. Continuing your exhalation, follow this with the 'mm' for ten seconds.

4. Repeat the chanting for five minutes.

5. After chanting, refocus on your breathing for a further minute and hold in your mind a contented image to end the exercise.

Surprisingly, according to research conducted at the University of Kansas, the interface between physical health and positive emotions is even more critical than having our physical bodily needs, such as adequate nutrition and shelter, met. This is why people with a positive mindset can overcome trials and deprivations, which appear totally unendurable, such as being lost for days at sea. We can harness this ability to great effect in less dramatic situations, such as awaiting test results or before attending an important interview.

PART TWO:
Wakefulness and well-being

6. Building a healthy approach to life

The mind is its own place, and in itself
Can make a Heav'n of Hell, a Hell of Heav'n.

John Milton, *Paradise Lost*, Book I, 254-5

Nobody's life is totally stress-free, and how we respond to the inevitable difficulties of life's curve balls is key to our level of positive well-being. Your attitude and approach to life is fundamental to whether or not you commit to creating this positive well-being. Consequently, this chapter on attitude precedes chapters on eating a healthy diet, exercising regularly and finding time for relaxation and sleep. If you don't feel empowered, worthy and competent, then it is unlikely that you will be proactive in seeking a healthy, balanced life. This chapter includes ten key steps, which provide the mental scaffolding on which sound foundations for positive well-being can be constructed.

The wise among us don't wait until our fence has rotted before applying creosote to protect it or let our car tyres become dangerously low before filling them up with air. Proactively embracing these ten habits will not totally inoculate you from life's difficulties, but it will reduce their frequency, since many problems are self-induced, and, more importantly, will enable you to handle them with greater resourcefulness and resilience. You will learn not only to anticipate problems, thus preventing or mitigating damage, but also to choose the life you wish to live, by following your inclinations and aspirations. This list of key practices will provide you with the necessary structure for building a healthy approach to life.

1. Adopt an attitude of gratitude
2. Forgive
3. Value your relationships
4. Live in your element
5. Invest in others
6. Focus on experiences
7. Take risks and accept challenges
8. Embrace humour
9. Let optimism be your default stance
10. Conclude each day with positive reflections.

These practices will enable you to meet your basic emotional needs, as discussed in chapter 4, and to move towards discovering your true self, as described by Carl Rogers (see p. 25). Try the following exercise to establish how well you are looking after your mental attitude.

 How healthy is your attitude to life? Scan the list of key practices and rate how well you look after yourself with regard to each concept on a scale of 0–10. Ten means that you address this area to the maximum, and zero means that you totally neglect this aspect of your life. Any area that scores less than five would benefit from being worked on. Any score of three or less requires immediate attention. If your total score is 90 plus, with no particular concept dropping below an eight, you have my hearty congratulations. If not, this chapter will help you to assess areas for improvement.

Now, let's explore each of these concepts in turn and see how you can apply them to the way you live your life.

1. Adopt an attitude of gratitude

Look at what you've got and make the best of it. It is better to light a candle than to curse the dark.

Proverb

An attitude of gratitude means looking at what we have rather than bewailing the deficits in our lives. It is about recognizing how far we have come, rather than permanently looking at how far we have to go. This practice involves celebrating our successes, good fortune, strengths and relationships.

You can cultivate this positive attitude with simple exercises like enumerating ten things that you appreciate about your life before you get up in the morning. This will set your day off to a positive start and pre-empt negative thoughts about the weather or the day's tasks.

It doesn't reduce your workload, but it can help you to

handle the day better if you aren't feeling despondent and defeated before you even start. Plus, by exuding a cheerful aura you will find that your colleagues and family will be much more willing to help and support you. People do not like to consort with those whose bad mood pulls them down.

As well as being grateful for what you have, it is a healthy practice to appreciate other people's good fortune too, since delighting in their achievements and triumphs enables you to feel vicariously positive. You will have experienced this when the football team you support wins a match or your fellow countryman wins a medal at the Olympics.

2. Forgive

Some people think it's holding that makes
one strong – sometimes it's letting go.
Anonymous

Harbouring resentment has a cost and you land up footing the bill. By letting go of hurts from the past, you free up energy for more constructive purposes. Whoever has offended you, or let you down in some way, has already robbed you in terms of your trust or self-esteem. Regardless of the damage done, try to draw a line under the hurt; otherwise you are bound in a negative way to that person for life. As Oscar Wilde playfully advised: 'Always forgive your enemies – nothing annoys them so much.' Don't give the perpetrator the satisfaction of a lifelong dividend for their actions by paying further with your emotions.

It is also vital that we learn to forgive ourselves. Many of us find this far more difficult to achieve. Holding onto guilt about a previous action eats away at your self-esteem and inner peace. Remember that we are all imperfect human beings; so treat yourself and others with compassion when mistakes are made.

3. Value your relationships

Friendships play a considerable role in engendering positive well-being. We have a basic emotional need to give and receive attention (see p. 40) in order to prevent loneliness, receive comfort and share our joys. It is instinctive to want to spend time with people in whom we trust and who accept us for who we are.

A good friendship is a reciprocal arrangement in which both parties attend to these needs. If a friendship is a one-way street, with one person doing all the giving and the other all the taking, it is worse than no friendship at all. These toxic relationships sap our energy and dash our expectations. It is imperative that this type of relationship be addressed. If it proves not to be salvageable, then sack the so-called friend before further harm is caused to your sense of well-being.

To be a good friend it helps to be forgiving, and willing to listen and invest time in nurturing the relationship. Also, remember that as you age your needs and interests change;

this is not a problem if you adapt your friendship groups accordingly. Many people who were happy to be the class clown feel uncomfortable about being serious when they are older and seeking companionship which respects this quality. Never allow yourself to be stuck in a rut, and surround yourself with friendship groups that can support you at every changing stage in your development.

Intimate relationships

A strong, loving relationship with a partner provides all the benefits of a friendship and so much more. If this relationship is working well and you feel loved, it is a most powerful experience, which will recharge your batteries and go a long way to meeting your emotional needs. In addition, the physical affection shown in intimate relationships causes the release of the hormone, oxytocin, which strengthens the attachment between partners. Do you ensure that your partner knows that you love them as they are, regardless of their achievements and successes? This links in with Carl Rogers' concept of unconditional positive regard (see p. 33) where we love, esteem and accept a person for who they are, without conditions.

TRY IT NOW! Think about your intimate relationship and ask yourself if you offer each other sufficient time, space, fun, support, trust, honesty, respect, freedom, equality and affection. If anything is missing from this list, then the sooner it is rectified the happier you both will be. Try to be honest with yourself and ask if you are jealous, demanding and manipulative or see your partner as a means to acquire wealth, status or other opportunities. If the latter is the case, you are not only exploiting them but also robbing yourself of the experience of totally being in tune with another person. As in all successful relationships, honest, assertive (but kind) communication is essential.

4. Live in your element

Living in your element means doing something that feels just right. When we experience being in our element we feel competent and totally engaged in our chosen activity (or inactivity) and contented in our surroundings. This can be something that is familiar, like skiing or dancing when the moves seem to come naturally, enabling us to perform with unconscious competence. It can also be something that is unfamiliar, such as experimenting with a more advanced dive, visiting a new country or embarking upon an adventure.

Being in your element can cover absolutely any practice. I have witnessed people being in their element when:

- Listening to their favourite music
- Dancing ecstatically
- Solving a puzzle, crossword or Sudoku
- Playing bridge
- Enjoying a gourmet meal

- Watching football
- Decorating a cake
- Floating on a lilo
- Playing hockey
- Creating a flower arrangement
- Reading a book by their favourite author
- Singing in a choir
- Cheering at a boat race
- Painting a picture
- Playing a musical instrument
- Relaxing with a friend in a comfortable chair with a cup of tea
- Driving a motorbike
- Having a snooze in a hammock
- Enjoying a film
- Writing a report
- Taking a romantic stroll along the beach
- Washing the car.

As you can see from this diverse list, many different things turn people on. Some are exciting and some are quite sedentary. It really doesn't matter as long as you enjoy whatever it is you are doing and feel comfortable in your own skin. We often feel guilty or self-indulgent about taking these pleasures and yet by doing them we really increase our overall sense of well-being. By discovering what it is that makes your heart sing you release endorphins into the body, and these feel-good hormones are like a natural tonic to improve your health and vitality. This is because participating in activities such as sports, which expose us to sunlight and exercise, causes the release of our happiness hormone, serotonin. This release of endorphins and serotonin not only makes us more fun to be around, but also gives us more energy to help others.

As with everything else in life, moderation is key. I am not suggesting we watch football incessantly or scoff endless meals! Make it your intention to do something you enjoy on a daily basis.

THINK ABOUT IT When were you last in your element, experiencing that total sense of synergy that results from being fully present in the moment, doing something that you feel born to do? If your response to this question is fairly recently, then well done. If not, think back to when you last felt really contented, joyful or fulfilled. What were you doing? Perhaps your views have changed, or maybe you are not physically able to participate in your previous hobby. Whatever the situation, ask yourself, if you were given a three-month sabbatical, how would you spend that time to achieve maximum fulfilment? Let your answer be a guide towards living in your element.

---

5. Invest in others

> If you want to lift yourself up, lift up someone else.
> Booker T. Washington

We all know the buzz we get when we invest in others, be it our children, partner, friends, family or colleagues. To witness the unbridled joy of a child when they master a skill we have been teaching them, such as swimming or riding a bicycle, is such a wonderful experience. This pleasure also works just as effectively if you go beyond your immediate gene pool or acquaintances and offer help to a total stranger.

It doesn't even have to cost you financially since kind gestures can be free. A smile, a friendly nod or a few words of encouragement can make the loneliest and most isolated soul feel that little bit better. You will recall that we have a basic emotional need to give and receive attention. We also have a need for status or to feel appreciated by others (see p. 40).

THINK ABOUT IT When did you last reach out to someone with compassion or simply give someone a well-deserved compliment? Such acts not only enrich the recipient but you too receive a reward, since your brain releases the bonding hormone oxytocin, which in turn activates the brain's pleasure and reward system.

CASE STUDY

Recently a friend informed me that someone close to her, whom she greatly respected, had just been awarded his UK citizenship. She invited all her friends and family to acknowledge his achievement – of passing the exams and other requirements – by sending him congratulatory emails. This recognition meant the world to the new citizen and really endorsed his sense of welcome and belonging to his adopted country. I have no doubt that my friend also gained great pleasure from bringing this recognition about and witnessing his appreciation and happiness as a result of her thoughtful act.

Rosie Swale Pope, an ordinary person, embraced this principle of investing in others to the ultimate. On the death of her husband from a cancer that might have been cured if caught early enough, she began investing in others. She ran round the world to raise awareness of the importance of health checks, while fundraising for this and many other causes. As a consequence, she not only enhanced her own well-being but that of numerous others too.

TRY IT NOW!

What can you do to give someone a lift today? It could be as simple as greeting someone who walks your way, helping a colleague at work or assisting somebody who is weighed down with luggage. It might be offering a listening ear to a friend or offering directions to someone who appears lost. You could make a larger investment, such as raising funds for a charity. Maybe you could give regular time to a local school to assist children who need extra support with their reading and writing. The possibilities for doing small or large acts of kindness are endless.

---

6. Focus on experiences

A friend once bought me an embroidered cushion, which she said expressed how she thinks of me. The caption on the cushion read: 'Life is too short, so let's have pudding first.'

These amusing words conceal a profound message for our well-being. From childhood we have learnt that puddings are a treat, which we are allowed to have as a reward for having eaten the sensible and nutritious part of the meal, i.e. the meat and greens. We often get bound up in our responsibilities and duties and lose track of the fun side of life. The key is to adopt an attitude of flexibility and to capitalize on the opportunities offered. For example, we cannot always guarantee what kind of weather we are going to get and, should a glorious sunny day unexpectedly present itself, allow yourself to abandon non-urgent plans to take advantage of the situation without experiencing guilt.

I am not for one minute advocating that you behave irresponsibly, but sometimes doing the laundry or tidying up the kitchen can wait, and instead you can enjoy an unscheduled walk with a friend or have a game of tennis with your family. Some people have been so powerfully socialized with the concept of 'work first, then play' that they find it very difficult to abandon themselves to serendipitous opportunities. Remember reliability and spontaneity are both virtues and there is a time and place for both in a balanced approach towards life. Are you being held back by a condition of worth that prevents you from seizing what the moment has to offer?

We can also become slaves to providing material possessions for our families and forget that it is the experiences that are the real treasures. Photograph albums are full of pictures relating to holidays, adventures and rites of passage. Although material comforts are important too, I am sure you will agree that people seldom fill their albums with shots of the fridge-freezer, loft insulation or the new bathroom tiles.

How do we focus on experiences?

First, we can stop being overly concerned about how others might regard us and cut out non-essential chores. Is it really necessary to iron underwear, dust and vacuum daily or have the grass permanently looking manicured?

Second, lower your standards of perfection and your budget. I have noticed that the people in the members' areas at Henley Regatta or Ascot Racecourse, frequently do not appear to be having half as good a time as those picnicking in the car parks. There is far more atmosphere 'up in the gods', on the last night of the BBC Proms concerts than you would find in any of the more expensive seats. In fact, since the advent of corporate hospitality, the real enthusiasts are usually in the cheap seats at sporting or cultural events. If you always wait to do something in style, you may miss the boat altogether.

Third, avoid wastage. Look at the excessiveness of our food and other purchases at Christmas and throughout the year. Unless you never throw away any unused food and wear every garment you have ever purchased, you are guilty of this practice. Work out what is enough and don't keep changing the goal posts for bigger and better. Surplus cash can then be used for enjoying time with your family and friends.

Fourth, we can develop an adventurous attitude towards all opportunities that come our way. Adopt a default position of 'have a go' or 'don't be afraid to try something new'. After all, you won't know if you would like something until you try. It is only by taking risks that we grow and evolve, so stop being frightened by the possibility of failure and become excited about the prospect of new horizons, joy and success. Your attitude towards embracing new experiences is akin to an umbrella, utterly useless when closed.

Give some thought to your daily routines and eliminate all superfluous activity; this will enable you to reclaim valuable time to enjoy more experiences, thus providing your life with deeper richness and greater interest.

7. Take risks and accept challenges

Begin, be bold and venture to be wise.

Horace

If rest and relaxation prevents *burn-out*, then having a challenge in life prevents *rust-out*. Burn-out is caused by too much stimulation – the demands made upon us outstrip our available resources, leading to exhaustion and anxiety. Rust-out is the opposite and is caused by insufficient stimulation, which engenders apathy and depression. As humans we need purpose and challenge in our lives. The brain initially rewards us when we achieve a skill but then gradually diminishes this reward to spur us on to greater proficiency.

Think back to the euphoria you experienced when you first learnt how to ride a bike or swim. Now, try to remember how long you enjoyed the buzz of that achievement of being able to doggy paddle before you were spurred on to master the crawl. Satisfaction is always short-lived, so we continually strive to improve our speed or style in order to re-experience the exhilaration of mastery.

Furthermore, when we are stretched to meet challenges, we actually increase certain brain cells. Sadly, when we allow ourselves to become overly stressed and our resources cannot meet the demands put upon us, we actually kill off brain cells. It is for this reason that psychologists eternally talk about achieving balance in life. In addition, recent research has identified that learning a new language or playing a musical instrument may reduce your susceptibility to developing dementia or may delay its onset. There is so much to gain from being open to developing new skills and interests.

No matter what type of challenge you choose, the key factor is just to feel stretched in some purposeful way. Appropriate challenges are unique to each individual and, of course, should be achievable, or they will only generate stress. There is no point in setting yourself the challenge of becoming an Olympic runner when you are 88 years old or becoming a heavyweight champion boxer when you have a slight build. Here are a dozen ideas offering possible challenges:

- Enrol on a course of study
- Try a new hobby
- Delete unwanted emails
- Master a new instrument
- Learn how to cook
- File things properly so you can find them
- Cut down on your salt intake
- Visit new countries
- Get up earlier and visit the gym
- Give up smoking
- Declutter your house
- Contact an old friend you have lost touch with.

Refuse to remain stagnant; harness your curiosity and strike out in life – seek the unknown territory that lies beyond your comfort zone to discover your ever-unfolding, remarkable potential.

8. Embrace humour

They say that 'laughter is the best medicine', and there is an abundance of evidence to support this claim. Laughter is therapeutic because:

- It facilitates cardiovascular activity by increasing blood flow, and it improves blood vessel functionality, all of which protects the heart.

- It improves muscle relaxation by releasing muscle tension in the facial, abdominal and back areas, and this in turn reduces the stress signals sent to the brain. So you will always feel suppler after a hearty laughter work-out.

- It inhibits the release of stress hormones (e.g. adrenaline, cortisol) and increases the number of antibodies (e.g. T-cells, Gamma-interferon) released, which will boost your immune system, making you more resistant to disease and infection.

- It causes the release of endorphins – your body's feel-good chemicals. Endorphins not only make us feel happy and increase our confidence and sense of well-being, but they also act as powerful analgesics for pain relief. Laughter is by far the cheapest and most efficient mood-enhancer available.

- It is often shared with others so can help towards forging or strengthening bonds in relationships and promoting shared happiness.

- It can be used as a way of defusing tension in a difficult situation.

- Genuine laughter, as opposed to nervous laughter, is a very attractive and infectious commodity, which tends to draw people towards us. It sends out signals of confidence and spontaneity and shows a lack of defensiveness and inhibition.

- There is even evidence that laughter increases memory, alertness, the ability to learn and creativity, according to research conducted at The Johns Hopkins University School of Medicine.

Ask yourself these questions:
- Do I smile a lot?
- Do I make time in my day for laughter?

If you find that daily laughter eludes you, you are probably not making enough time for 'play'. Try to ensure that you have some unserious companions and invest the time to play with pets, children, partners and friends. Think about who and what makes you smile, since smiling is usually a precursor to laughter.

We are all unique when it comes to what tickles our fancy; however, if you have lost touch with your funny bone, you might find some of the following ideas useful to put you back on track towards enjoying laughter: watch comedies, read humorous books, play games, don a fancy dress outfit, put on face paints or have a pillow or water pistol fight.

9. Let optimism be your default stance

Make the best of what is in your power
and take the rest as it happens.

Epictetus

According to research, optimistic people live considerably longer than their pessimistic counterparts. This is because optimism reduces stress levels, blood pressure, cholesterol and the chance of heart disease and has many more health benefits. Optimism radically enhances the way we live our daily lives since in its wake follows: resourcefulness, creativity, hope, greater productivity, improved social life, happier moods, greater motivation, higher levels of satisfaction and greater confidence.

An **optimist** is someone whose default disposition is to look on the bright side of life. They seek out favourable outcomes, unlike a **pessimist**, who tends to routinely anticipate the worst eventualities.

I like to think of optimism and pessimism as our inner climate. In the same way that warm sunshine can make us eager to be out and about, and a cold, grey start to the day can make us feel flat and cheerless, so too can a bright or gloomy disposition change the entire complexion of the day.

By consciously changing our attitude to life to an optimistic one we can tap into our inner resources far more effectively and make more friends along the way. It will come as no surprise to you that the company of optimists is more sought after than that of pessimists.

There is an old argument that by expecting the worst, you will be relieved when it doesn't happen or prepared if it does. This is not sound. The brain works on expectations, and – thanks to belief in a negative outcome – you will be less resilient to meet this eventuality should it arise. This, of course, is linked to the concept of self-fulfilling prophecy. Next time you have a job interview, if you indoctrinate yourself that you will fail miserably, the chances are that you won't even be short-listed. However, if you feed your brain a diet of optimistic thoughts, you will create positive, empowering beliefs in your ability to handle life and to make the right choices. After all, behind every success story lies a person who believed in themselves.

Pessimism can result in a negative cycle of worry, poor sleep, a weakened immune system and a lack of resourcefulness in dealing with challenges and disappointments. The optimist will be much more likely to dust themself down and move on, confident in the knowledge that the situation is only temporary. They will then have the necessary motivation, energy and resources to try again or plot another way forward.

Are you an optimist or a pessimist? Perhaps you treat some situations you encounter with optimism and others with pessimism. Can you identify the reasons for your prevailing attitudes? You may be able to trace a pessimistic disposition back to a powerful negative experience from the past. If this is blighting a particular area of your life, you can seek help from a human givens therapist who will be able to de-traumatize you by means of what is known as the 'rewind technique' (see p. 39 for more on the human givens approach).

Another cause of a pessimistic outlook is cognitive distortions, which are unhelpful thinking styles. For example, do you have a tendency to catastrophize situations, focus on the negative information and filter out the positive or take things personally when they are meant as generalizations? Recognizing pessimistic thought patterns and intercepting them immediately is important to prevent a negative belief system from becoming established. Ask yourself where the evidence is to support this belief. By continually challenging pessimistic habits you will start to develop new ways to meet everyday situations more positively and rationally, enabling you to create an optimistic outlook towards life.

IF YOU REMEMBER ONE THING Having an optimistic outlook sets you off to a flying start in life by being able to deal resource-fully with whatever comes your way, be it adversity or opportunities. Make a promise to yourself today to cultivate this disposition, which will significantly contribute towards enhancing your positive well-being.

10. Conclude each day with positive reflections

In the same way that you start each day with an attitude of gratitude, it is wise to conclude the day by reflecting on at least three things which have made you happy. If you struggle to find three sources of pleasure, here are a few ideas to get you started:

- Planning a holiday
- Sharing a laugh with a colleague
- Finding a bargain
- Enjoying a good book
- Snuggling up on the sofa with a good DVD
- Receiving a hug
- Enjoying a relaxing bath
- Receiving an invitation in the post
- Enjoying a great night out with your partner
- Meeting a deadline on time
- Lighting a scented candle
- Hearing an inspirational speech.

Doing this daily exercise enables you to acknowledge the simple joys in life, rather than hurtling through your day without noticing them. In the same way that art connoisseurs develop their appreciation of art by studying the finer details of artworks, you will learn to take satisfaction from the little things. This will inevitably positively impact on your well-being, which in turn will make you more resilient to stress.

THINK ABOUT IT The ten tips covered in this chapter cost nothing to implement and, if adopted, will radically improve your positive well-being. Return to the exercise at the start of this chapter and begin to work on each area where your score was low. Remember that the brain works on expectations; by expecting positive outcomes you will significantly enhance your quality of life.

7. Exercise and fitness

Health is defined by the World Health Organization (WHO) as 'a state of complete physical, mental and social well-being and not merely the absence of disease and infirmity'. We have already touched on the positive effects of endorphins and serotonin – released when we exercise – and most of us will have been frequently told that exercise is essential for good physical and mental health. Yet many of us do very little about putting this advice into practice. Exercise is beneficial for everyone regardless of age or ability. If you exercise regularly, then congratulate yourself on the good work and keep it up. For those of you who have not tried exercising before, remember that it is *never* too late to learn. The improvement in your positive well-being will rapidly make you appreciate the value of incorporating this activity into your daily routine.

Benefits of exercise

There is a veritable avalanche of studies on the benefits of exercise. The general medical consensus is that exercise:

1. Increases life expectancy
2. Reduces the risk of a stroke
3. Lowers the risk of heart disease
4. Lowers the risk or slows down the onset of dementia
5. Reduces the risk of breast and colon cancers

6. Lowers the risk of osteoarthritis and osteoporosis
7. Increases self-esteem
8. Boosts energy levels
9. Manages weight
10. Lowers stress levels
11. Elevates mood
12. Lowers the risk of type 2 diabetes
13. Enhances quality of sleep
14. Boosts good cholesterol
15. Improves body tone
16. Strengthens joints, muscles and bones
17. Prevents constipation
18. Reduces the risk of suffering from depression
19. Prevents impotence
20. Reduces levels of aggression.

The simple message is that it really does work.

Sitting-Rising Test (SRT)

A simple way to check your fitness is to stand bare-footed on the floor and then lower yourself into a sitting position. The easiest way to do this is to cross your legs. If you can do this in a controlled manner using just your feet then award yourself five points. For each extra part of the body you use (e.g. knee, hand or forearm), deduct a point from your maximum five-point score. For example, if you need to use two hands to support yourself to sit down then reduce your score to three.

Now, from the sitting position, try to stand up unaided. As before, award yourself five points for an unassisted movement and deduct a point for each additional body part that you need to use. If you have to rock on your back to propel yourself up, remember to deduct a point. The overall exercise is worth ten points.

Because this simple exercise involves body flexibility, balance, musculoskeletal tone, coordination and strength, it is an excellent indicator of overall fitness and has proved to be a useful test for predicting physical well-being and longevity. If you have scored poorly (less than eight), improve your physical fitness by exercising.

How to design your exercise routine

We can all afford the time if we see exercise as a priority

You can reap these benefits for the modest investment of approximately 22 minutes of moderate exercise per day. You can do traditional 'work-out' exercises, such as sit-ups, squats or press-ups. However, if the thought of gyms and dumbbells puts you off, it is perfectly adequate to go for a brisk walk, dance, play tennis, cycle or swim vigorously. If you really want to capitalize on limited time, you can achieve an increase in heart rate while doing your chores, such as mowing the lawn, cleaning your windows or vacuuming the carpet with a degree of urgency.

Alternatively if you are truly pressed for time, eleven

minutes per day of intense exercise will raise your heart rate to such an extent that you will achieve the same health rewards in half the time. For those of you who have a little more time to spare, you can aim for a mixture of the two and spend eleven minutes doing moderate exercise followed by six minutes of intense exercise.

Make your fitness schedule a priority, a definite commitment, by setting aside time each day for exercising. This may be at a regular time or dependent upon the activity if it involves a class. Try to ensure that it is not first thing in the morning or last thing at night. Studies have shown that your metabolism yields more benefits from the release of endocrine hormones such as cortisol if you exercise later on in the day. However, exercising late at night will interfere with your ability to sleep, so late afternoon or early evening are good times to set aside for your fitness regimen.

How to get started

Try to incorporate a range of activities consisting of aerobic and resistance exercises. The resistance or strengthening exercises help to build up muscle density and protect against bone loss. Lifting weights, heavy gardening, carrying shopping or suitcases all help to make your muscles leaner. Aerobic or cardio exercises increase your heart rate and build up cardiovascular endurance or stamina. Cycling, using a cross trainer, walking briskly or running, particularly uphill, are all examples of aerobic exercise. Try to vary these exercises so that all muscle groups are strengthened.

A good rule of thumb, when designing your exercise routine, is to start with gentle resistance exercises or stretches, moving on to the more demanding aerobic exercises; then return to the strengthening exercises. I refer to this as the 'aerobic sandwich', and this schedule is an easy way to cover the warm-up and cool-down aspects of your exercise plan.

REMEMBER THIS!!! Respect and listen to your body. Do a gentle warm-up, which will gradually stretch your muscles and increase your heart rate, and end with a gentle cool-down to acclimatize your body to a slower pace. If you feel pain, do not continue to exercise, since this is your body's way of telling you that you are at risk of doing damage. You should only experience mild tension when stretching muscles and must not go beyond this point.

If you have neglected your physical fitness, do not suddenly launch into vigorous exertion, but build up endurance gradually by increasing the time and difficulty of your chosen exercise incrementally. Regular exercising is a fundamental lifestyle change that you will need to maintain continuously. If you strain yourself by overdoing it initially, you are unlikely to continue. Slowly but surely is the way to make exercising maintainable, by setting small realistic goals.

1   Learn how to breathe correctly when exercising since this will increase the benefits of the activity. Taking a course in Pilates, yoga or tai chi are excellent ways to optimize your breathing. In general you should breathe in when increasing the tension of your muscles and breathe out as you release that tension and relax.

2. Stay well hydrated while exercising by having a bottle of water to hand and take frequent, small sips. It is not advisable to rapidly gulp a lot of water, since this might make you feel nauseous or disrupt your workout.

3. Before embarking on an exercise programme, check with your GP if you have any health concerns – such as: previous injuries; suffer from obesity; have a heart condition; are pregnant; have had recent surgery.

4. Don't exercise if you are feeling ill.

Enjoy yourself

If your chosen form of exercise does not give you intrinsic pleasure then it is unlikely that you will persist in doing it. To retain your motivation level, play your favourite music, listen to a radio programme you enjoy or exercise with friends to turn it into a more sociable pursuit. You may also be able to hold yourself to the commitment more if you involve others, so if you can't get a friend involved, you might try attending a class regularly.

If possible, choose an activity that is outdoors, as you will reap even more benefits from your exercise. An abundance of studies show that connecting with nature promotes a state of positive well-being. This is due, in part, to avoiding indoor pollution, increasing our vitamin D intake from sunlight and the calming impact of natural scenes. There is no doubt that outdoor activity can confer spiritual, mental and physical benefits. Why not try it?

 To make your exercising sustainable, discover what you really enjoy doing so that you look forward to the activity. You may discover that you are a team player who will enjoy sports like hockey, football or netball. If you prefer more solitary pursuits then running, swimming or gym workouts might suit you better, particularly if you use this time to contemplate and de-stress yourself after interaction with others.

We trade in health for convenience

In addition to our struggle to dedicate time to exercise, today we perform a number of tasks with the assistance of machines, reducing our opportunities to move – whether it's using the car to get around, or the vacuum cleaner or electric mixer in the home. Giving up the gadgets and manually performing tasks like kneading bread or even brushing your teeth can have a surprising, positive effect on your health. Although these tasks in themselves may seem inconsequential in terms of physical expenditure of energy, the aggregate figure is quite significant.

One study concerning sedentariness in office workers revealed that having office chairs on wheels played a big part in diminishing the level of physical activity in employees. The study showed that workers would seldom get up to file documents but would simply propel themselves to filing cabinets and back to their desks, remaining seated throughout. In a short space of time, this was reflected in the extra weight that employees gained.

Use it or lose it

Take every small opportunity to move around more in order to burn off energy, and try to avoid being sedentary for too long, such as sitting in front of the TV or computer screen. Increase your activity and decrease the amount of time you spend sitting and lying down. This will not only help with weight control but will significantly reduce your chances of developing a number of chronic diseases. When you're at work, simple things, like regular visits to the drinking fountain, taking a stroll during your lunch break or visiting a colleague's office rather than picking up the phone, can make a big difference. Capitalize on your daily commute by parking your car a little further away from the station so that you build in a regular ten minute walk there and back. When returning home, don't just slump onto a chair, but instead retain your momentum by doing your household chores, walking the dog or doing yoga.

REMEMBER THIS!!! Keep in mind why you are exercising: it is good for the brain, improves your mood and sleep quality, and ensures that your body remains supple, mobile and healthy.

8. Eating well

Eat well, drink in moderation and sleep sound,
In these three good health abound.

Latin Proverb

A massive contributor to our positive well-being is what we eat and drink. The benefits of healthy eating are great in terms of our physical, mental and emotional state. A healthy diet increases our energy levels and resistance to diseases, enables us to recover more swiftly from injuries and illnesses and facilitates the management of chronic health problems. Perhaps most significantly, from a physical health point of view, it can substantially prolong our lifespan and, even more importantly, our increased longevity can be active and fulfilling.

From a mental health stance, adequate nourishment plays a significant role in increasing our concentration levels and general mental acuity, improving our alertness and ability to learn new skills and enabling us to memorize and retrieve information. Our food consumption also plays a vital role in moderating our mood, levels of anxiety and susceptibility to depression. Without vital minerals, vitamins and other nutrients we cannot feel happy and fulfilled, since the hormones which enable us to experience these positive emotions cannot be naturally manufactured by the body if the basic nutritional building blocks are absent.

THINK ABOUT IT

A child who is hungry or sleep deprived is usually not good news and will freely show signs of irritability, aggressiveness and fractiousness. Adults are no different, although we may endeavour to conceal it. Without adequate nutrition, the essential fuel for our brain and body, we too will perform under par, become ill-adjusted and are unlikely to be a joy to live with.

Food and body image

Many people in today's society have missed the point that food is a means to nourishment, energy and positive well-being and instead see food consumption as exclusively linked to body image. Clearly this is a triumph of form over function, since it is utterly contrary to our evolutionary imperatives.

The media and dieting industries have manipulated many of us with fat-shaming tactics, although much of the propaganda peddled is utterly false. Strong evidence supports the claim that metabolic fitness is a far more accurate barometer of health than weight. Many people who are considered 'overweight' according to their BMI are at no greater health risk than those deemed to be of 'normal' weight, provided that they are metabolically fit. The other side of the coin is that there are a number of slim people who are not metabolically fit, but they remain at risk because their low weight provides a false sense of security.

THINK ABOUT IT

Looks will inevitably fade, but a sharp brain, strong body and a happy disposition will afford you so much more joy and pleasure throughout your lifetime. Don't compromise these real treasures by kowtowing to prevailing body fashions.

Unsustainable diets do not work. By unsustainable I am referring to any diet that does not meet your long-term nutritional needs. They are not only unhealthy, boring and sometimes expensive but can actually cause a great deal of physical and mental harm. There is an abundance of evidence that repeated yo-yo dieting leads to ultimate weight increase for the vast majority of dieters. Radically reducing your calorie intake causes the body to invoke emergency starvation mode. This actually results in increased fat storage, since your brain reasons that you might have need of it later, if regular meals are not forthcoming. Each time you repeat the pattern of severe calorie reduction the brain instructs the body to downshift your metabolism and preserve as much fat as possible.

In some cases the severe malnutrition caused by extreme diets results in organ failure, loss of bone density and other serious health problems. Dieting can also trigger eating disorders, particularly anorexia nervosa: a silent killer that has claimed many lives, especially among the younger population.

Basic measurements for healthy eating

Calories

Calories are a measure of the energy content of food and drink. According to the National Health Service (NHS) in the UK, the average man should consume approximately 2,500 calories per day and the average woman 2,000 in order to maintain their weight. Bear in mind that these are only averages and if you are built like Hugh Jackman then this figure might need to be significantly higher than if built like Benedict Cumberbatch (both popular actors).

If you consume more calories than you burn off (energy expenditure), you will put on weight; conversely if you burn more calories than you consume, you will lose weight. When we suffer from obesity due to our energy expenditure being significantly less than our calorie consumption, we increase our risk of type 2 diabetes, stroke, heart disease and various cancers.

As well as considering your build and size, it is important to look at other factors when working out the amount of calories you should consume. Important considerations include your age, lifestyle (how active or sedentary you are), hormone balance, medication intake and current state of health. It is worth noting that your metabolism slows down every year once you reach your 40s. This means that even if you maintain your activities and food intake to the exact same levels as during your 20s and 30s, you will put on weight. You must therefore either decrease your food intake or increase your exercise regimen in order to maintain your previous weight.

BMI and other measures

A basic tool to work out if you are consuming the correct quantity of food and drink (calories) to match the amount of calories you burn as a result of your lifestyle (degree of activity) is your *body mass index* (BMI). BMI is a measure of the body's mass, based on weight and height. It is calculated by dividing a person's weight in kilograms by the square of their height in metres. The ideal BMI for men and women falls within the range of 18.5–24.9. If you are below that you are considered to be underweight, and above that, overweight. In addition the BMI guidelines vary by ethnicity; for example, the 'normal' ranges of a Caucasian BMI are significantly higher than those recommended for those of Asian ethnicity, based on average build and risk of contracting diseases like diabetes.

REMEMBER THIS!!! The BMI can be a useful indicator that you need to make changes to your diet and exercise regimen. However, remember that it is a very blunt instrument, designed for populations rather than individuals, which should not be used in isolation. It is more accurate for those of an average height and build, but can be particularly inaccurate when applied to very tall or muscular people.

Another simple way to ascertain a healthy body shape according to the UK's NHS is to ensure that your waist measurement does not expand beyond a certain size – 31.5 inches (80 cm) in women and 37 inches (94 cm) in men. Remember that these measurements are based on averages; don't worry if you exceed them slightly. If your measurements are markedly in excess of these measurements, you will be at a greater risk of developing problems with your health. If you are carrying extra weight, it is far better that this weight is distributed around the hips, buttocks and thighs than the waist area. A wealth of evidence exists which demonstrates the close link between this kind of weight – known as 'central obesity' and resulting from excess visceral fat – and type 2 diabetes, cardiovascular disease and Alzheimer's disease, among other illnesses. Address this by increasing exercise and decreasing calorie intake, or a combination of the two.

Age

Our ability to digest and process vital vitamins and minerals diminishes with age due to the reduction in saliva and stomach acid production. Older people can become mentally less alert and memory retrieval can become more unreliable due to deficiencies in folic acid or vitamin B. It is helpful to increase your fibre consumption to address this problem. Fibre comes from plants and is either soluble or insoluble; both types are beneficial to the body. Root vegetables, fruit, barley and oats are good soluble sources, and bran, nuts, wholemeal bread and seeds are excellent insoluble sources.

As we get older, it is also advisable to reduce salt intake (to prevent high blood pressure and water retention), increase calcium intake (to improve bone density) and add more complex carbohydrates, such as beans, vegetables, whole grains and fruit – not fruit juice – (to help stabilize insulin levels).

Balancing your diet

The standard health advice is to eat a 'balanced diet', which means: eat a range of foods, incorporating fruit and vegetables; dairy; sources of protein such as fish, meat, eggs and beans; starchy foods such as potatoes, pasta and bread; and healthy fats, which lower cholesterol levels and are known as unsaturated, monounsaturated or polyunsaturated fats – found in nuts, olive and vegetable oil, avocados, seeds and fish. This is in contrast to trans-fats or saturated fats, which are found in things like pizzas, chips, chicken skin and candy bars, and which can cause high cholesterol and heart disease.

The latest research has shown that five portions (80g per portion) of vegetables and fruit daily provide the vital vitamins and minerals we require, alongside two portions of oily fish per week and a small quantity of meat. Meat in moderation is an excellent source of vitamins, such as vitamin B, and minerals, such as zinc and iron, as well as protein. However, it is recommended that we should adopt a vegetarian diet for at least two days a week, turning to protein sources such as soy products, nuts, beans and lentils. Filling your diet with a range of colourful fresh fruits and vegetables can significantly reduce your risk of stroke and heart disease, according to a wealth of studies.

High salt and sugar intake are commonplace in many Western diets and contribute to high blood pressure (which in turn increases your risk of heart disease or suffering a stroke), diabetes and other obesity-related illnesses. Try to limit your intake of both by steering away from processed foods and by flavouring your cooking with alternative seasonings, such as garlic, onions or other herbs.

Planning your meals

Plan your weekly menu so that it is interesting, varied and healthy, thereby ensuring that your nutritional requirements are met. Make a comprehensive shopping list and try to stick to this, although remember that labelling certain foods as 'forbidden' will only set up a craving for them, so allow the odd indulgence. Always operate with a degree of flexibility so that you can enjoy attending dinner parties or visits to restaurants without slavishly following 'food rules', which will not only make you feel deprived but may also irritate your hosts.

When shopping, stick to a few general rules to make it easier to choose healthy options and avoid going off-piste:

- Make the majority of your purchases fresh or frozen, and cut back on processed, pre-packaged or canned food.

- Try to shop when you are not hungry, since this will make you less likely to be seduced by marketing promotions that may not be in your best interests.

- Check food labels for hidden sugars, salts or unhealthy fats. Be suspicious if a label boasts that the contents are 'fat-free', since this usually means extra sugar or salt has been added to make it more palatable.

When it comes to preparing and eating your meals, invest sufficient time so that your food is appealing and enjoyable. This will make you less prone to resorting to fast foods or ready meals, which are seldom wholesome options. If you know that you get peckish in between meals, have a healthy stash of snacks available, such as nuts, fruit and vegetables. Be aware too of your eating environment. Try to eat your meals with a high degree of mindfulness. Rather than eating on the fly or grazing in front of the computer, sit down and focus on the taste and texture of your meal. Engaging all your senses will not only increase your enjoyment of the meal but will make you far less likely to eat too rapidly or over-eat.

Don't skip breakfast, as it serves to kick-start your metabolism and, for this reason, is the most important meal of the day. If you neglect breakfast, you not only deny yourself the necessary energy required to meet your working day but also increase the likelihood that your hunger will cause you to overeat later or fall prey to cravings for unhealthy convenience food. It is better to have lunch as your main meal of the day, but if this is not possible then ensure that your evening meal is not taken too late in the evening so that you do not go to bed on a full stomach.

 Avoid diets; they simply do not work, since if they did, you would only have to do it once, and this is seldom the case. Instead implement a tasty, nutritious and varied diet that is a sustainable and pleasurable lifestyle choice, and pay attention to your fitness level by incorporating exercise into your daily routine and ensuring you get the right amount of sleep.

Hydration

Since 60 per cent of our body composition is made up of water, it is imperative that we consistently replenish the water that is lost through natural bodily processes. Keep yourself well hydrated by drinking approximately eight glasses of fluids per day (8 × 8oz glass). This is, of course, general guidance only and will need to be varied in accordance with your level of physical activity, climate conditions and the state of your health, among other factors. Remember that water hydrates, whereas caffeinated or alcoholic drinks dehydrate the body.

It is advisable to take regular sips of water throughout the day rather than downing whole glasses rapidly. If you don't enjoy the taste of water, flavour it with fresh lemons, oranges, strawberries, kiwis or mangoes, the vitamins of which will give you an added boost to your immune system. These are just some of the reasons, supported by a wide range of studies, why a high level of hydration is critical to our well-being and general health. Hydration:

1. Boosts metabolism, facilitates digestion, transports nutrients to all the cells of the body and accelerates the rate at which we burn calories.

2. Reduces your risk of having a stroke or heart attack. It helps to thin the blood and reduces the risk of plaque build-up and blood clots.

3. Improves brain functioning enabling you to concentrate, be alert, less fatigued and more capable of making sensible decisions. It reduces the risk of suffering from headaches and makes you less prone to having accidents.

4. Keeps muscles moving and joints well lubricated and elastic enabling you to be less susceptible to injuries, cramps and strains. It also reduces the pain levels of chronic conditions such as arthritis. Water is essential for the necessary chemical reactions and the transportation of electrolytes to enable your muscles to contract and relax smoothly.

5. Plays an essential role in kidney functioning in flushing out toxins and prevents the formation of painful kidney

stones which are caused by a combination of dehydration, excess salt, fat, animal protein, alcohol and sugar intake.

6. Prevents cravings for snacks and has been shown to reduce food consumption at meals if a glass of water is drunk fifteen minutes before meal times. In this way it helps with weight control and obesity prevention.

7. Often improves skin tone and protects against premature skin ageing.

8. Boosts the immune system (cold water), facilitates relaxation and helps reduce stress (warm water), and helps to discharge toxins (steam).

THINK ABOUT IT It is not by accident that terms such as the Latin *aqua vitae* or the French *eau de vie* ('water of life') are so popular with manufacturers trying to emphasize the merits of their products, since water truly is essential for life. Staying adequately hydrated is one of the most important ingredients to positive well-being since it improves our physical, mental and emotional health.

Responding to emotional triggers

Learn to recognize emotional food triggers – such as anger, rejection, loneliness, stress and boredom – that may lead to comfort eating, which can become habitual. Many people use food as a reward, and most celebrations have food and drink as an intrinsic part of the occasion. This is absolutely fine as long as it falls within reasonable limits. Try to be aware of the various cues that have you heading for the biscuit tin or the wine bottle and replace this means of consolation or reward with a healthier strategy, such as a relaxing bath, watching a favourite film or visiting a friend. Equally, notice how you associate food with activities and venues and make sure that you do not indulge in these to excess. Does a week in Devon mean a lavish cream tea each afternoon or do you equate taking a flight as an opportunity to sink several gin and tonics, regardless of the time of day or night?

Additionally, beware of setting yourself emotional traps by following a poor diet. Effective neurotransmitter production is dependent upon a healthy, balanced diet. Neurotransmitters are chemicals made up of amino acids derived from your diet; they provide the building blocks for your natural mood-enhancers, helping to inoculate you from depression, anxiety, tension, low self-esteem, obsessiveness and irritability, among other negative moods. Brain chemicals like endorphins protect us from pain and help to increase positive feelings, and serotonin promotes sleep and diminishes our likelihood of feeling depressed.

Without a balanced and sufficiently caloric diet, we are not able to manufacture the full range of chemicals we need to stay well-adjusted. It not only seriously impacts upon your mood stability but can also make you a prime candidate for an eating disorder, and a raft of other physical and emotional problems. For example, a depletion of tryptophan, found in foods such as poultry and fish, causes serotonin levels to drop and this results in obsessive controlling behaviour, a hallmark of anorexia or bulimia nervosa. (See p. 159 for more on the effects of tryptophan and serotonin in regulating sleep.)

When choosing vegetables and fruits, remember that variety is essential to gain the full range of nutrients. Although dark leafy greens, like broccoli, kale and spinach, should be a staple of our diet since they are rich in vitamins and minerals, other coloured fruits and vegetables should not be neglected. Yellow peppers, orange carrots, red strawberries and tomatoes, blackberries, yellow melons and blueberries all contain different nutritional benefits and should be included. Different colours correspond to different nutrients, which is why it is advisable to keep menus varied. This will also add interest to meals making them more enjoyable as well as better for our health and well-being.

Listen to your body

Listen to your body and acknowledge its cues by eating when hungry and stopping when satisfied, and by drinking water regularly. Your body is naturally attuned to know the amount of food required, otherwise known as 'coordinating energy homeostasis'. It does this by releasing hunger signal hormones, such as ghrelin, and satiety signal hormones, such as leptin. These and other hormones monitor your body's needs, providing you do not interfere with their operation by neglecting to eat, exercise or sleep appropriately. If you are suffering from discomfort – feel constipated, have a headache, or feel tired, thirsty, sluggish or confused – increase your water intake and ensure you are following a balanced diet.

 Learn to listen to your body and not society. Your body is the best judge of knowing when you are hungry and when you are full. Enjoy and accept the skin you are in. A healthy body is a blessing and should be cherished. It has a job to do and by offering it the correct nourishment you will enable it to serve you better and for longer.

---

9. Relaxation

When we are unable to find tranquillity within
ourselves, it is useless to seek it elsewhere.
Francois de La Rochefoucauld

Why relaxation is important

Relaxation is not an 'optional extra' if we wish to enjoy good health and positive well-being. It is an essential skill, enabling us to handle constructively the small, routine stressors that are part of everyday life – such as being caught in a traffic jam and late for an important appointment – as well as to deal with major life events – such as redundancy and bereavement, which stretch to the maximum our ability to cope. It is unrealistic to imagine that we can engage with life and not have to face stressful situations from time to time.

The more pressurized your existence, be it through having a high-powered job, difficult family dynamics or personal problems, the more crucial your ability to relax becomes. Relaxation techniques enable you to think calmly and clearly in difficult situations where maximum concentration and focus are needed. Ernest Hemingway coined the poetic term 'grace under pressure' to describe courage in his novel, *The Sun Also Rises*, and this expression has since been adopted widely to describe the ability to relax in tricky circumstances.

It is a false economy to neglect regular relaxation, since an unchallenged state of perpetual nervousness or anxiety takes its toll on our health and well-being. People who suffer from chronic stress levels consistently flood their body with stress hormones, which, if left unchecked, may lead to physical symptoms. These include tension backaches and migraines, and greater susceptibility to catching a cold or the flu, due to lower immunity levels. Worst of all are the debilitating psychological and emotional distresses that follow in the wake of unmitigated high arousal levels. This can result in decreased self-confidence, a tendency to overreact and generally feeling depressed or out of control. Constant worrying actively interferes with the rest and digest mode, an essential component for positive well-being.

Relaxation has been shown to reduce the following stress related conditions:

- Panic attacks, depression and anxiety

- Heartburn, irritable bowel syndrome and ulcers

- Insomnia

- Chronic pain and difficulties in childbirth

- Infertility, impotence, premenstrual and menopausal tension

- Psoriasis, acne, eczema, dermatitis and urticaria

- High blood pressure, heart disease, Raynaud's and angina

- Fibromyalgia, arthritis, epilepsy and multiple sclerosis

- Asthma, chronic obstructive airways disease and emphysema

- Diabetes mellitus, herpes simplex and rheumatoid arthritis.

The relaxation response

As discussed in chapter 5, relaxation is the antidote to a trigger-happy fight or flight (F or F) response. The relaxation response causes the opposite physiological and biochemical effects to the intense state of arousal of the F or F response, which is extremely energy-intensive. By down-shifting your metabolism into the relaxed state when the parasympathetic nervous system becomes dominant, you become more energy-efficient and are also able to exert conscious control over your life. Even as long ago as the 5th century BC it was recognized that relaxation played an essential part in maintaining our mental stability. The ancient Greek historian Herodotus wrote: 'If a man insisted always on being serious and never allowed himself a bit of fun and relaxation, he would go mad or become unstable without knowing it.'

By investing in regular relaxation we are able to recalibrate this vital survival response to make it less likely to fire off inappropriately, which causes unnecessary panic attacks. With consistent practice, the ability to relax becomes a valu-able life-enhancing tool, which will not only increase your enjoyment of life but will also enable you to be far more efficient and productive.

Modern living is frenetic

Today, in the developed world, we are subjected to an incredibly fast pace of life, and we need to make a conscious effort to find the time and space to relax and tune into *ourselves* rather than into external stimuli, the default mode for many of us. Many people have become uncomfortable in their own company and find solitude and a quiet environment intolerable. The need, or addiction, to be in constant touch with emails or social media has led to a reduction in self-reliance.

Some people experience withdrawal symptoms, such as intense agitation, if asked to switch off mobile phones, tablets, TVs or computers. They have become accustomed to a backdrop of constant noise, and silence is deafening to them. It is not dissimilar to a smoker being prohibited from having a cigarette. This non-stop, often non-essential activity steals from the downtime that your mind and body need in order to function optimally.

THINK ABOUT IT How dependent have you become on external stimuli? Do you get your phone out as soon as you sit down on public transport or feel uncomfortable leaving it in your bag when spending time with others, instead placing it in sight on the table, to make sure you don't 'miss' anything? When you get home from work, do you automatically turn the TV or radio on? By always being plugged in, you deprive yourself of the opportunity to just spend time with yourself and to reflect, observe and relax (see p. 39).

Lack of real communication

Having worked for almost 25 years with the UK's leading couple therapy agency, I have frequently encountered couples where an incessant use of technology has caused immense friction in their relationship. I have also seen the proliferation of cybersex, which is less than constructive to most couple relationships. What might appear as innocuous addictions – such as a computer game obsession, compulsion to bring work home, or a need to check the latest news or messages constantly, even while on holiday – lead to couples investing increasingly less time in each other, which inevitably impacts their level of closeness and intimacy. The neglected partner often describes this in similar terms to an affair, although in this case the 'other man/woman' cited, is a Blackberry or an iPad!

Technology can be a valuable tool to improve our quality of life, but, as always, it is about striking the right balance so that it benefits us and our relationships, rather than hindering them.

THINK ABOUT IT

When was the last time that you enjoyed sitting on your own or in companionable silence with your partner, feeling totally relaxed and at peace with yourself?

Relaxation is a skill

Unfortunately, the need to relax appears to correlate inversely with our ability to do so; for many it is a forgotten or poorly-developed skill or even is erroneously regarded as a form of self-indulgence. Some people view the prospect of having quality relaxation time through a prism of guilt, as though it were synonymous with laziness. Yet endless studies have shown that it rejuvenates and refreshes the brain and body by decreasing anxiety levels and restoring control. Contrary to what people often believe, relaxation is not a passive process but an active skill, with which we consciously choose to tone down our level of arousal.

TRY IT NOW!

Organizations invest huge sums of money in 'stress management' for their key personnel. Stress management is just commercial speak for learning how to relax, that is, to reduce arousal levels. The main thrust of such training advocates the importance of following these steps when feeling stressed:

1. Slow down, since anxiety causes us to act hastily, and this way we often make mistakes.

2. Stay in the moment. By focusing on the present we gain greater clarity, rather than catastrophizing with 'what if' questions about the future.

3. Learn to embrace and enjoy high-pressure situations by recognizing your ability to cope and remain relaxed. Remember that a positive attitude and confidence are everything.

4. Instantly take action when you start to feel pressurized by smiling (which sends a message to the brain that things are okay) and maintaining deep, slow, rhythmical breathing.

THINK ABOUT IT

How did we learn to feel guilty about fulfilling our basic needs? We have very much gone astray in knowing how to look after our minds and bodies. So many of us now experience guilt about what we eat and how we look, taking time to relax or even getting sufficient sleep. Both mental and physical ill health will escalate if we don't take proper care of our well-being.

We often mistake relaxation for indulging in leisure pursuits. Plonking yourself down in front of the TV or reading

your favourite book may be enjoyable and provide enter-
tainment, but they are not the same as relaxing. Studies
using brainwave monitoring show that practising relaxation
techniques induces alpha brain waves, which effect beneficial physiological and biochemical changes. Relaxation
involves a decrease in heart rate, muscle activity and rate
of breathing as well as engendering a heightened state of
calmness and clarity. This does not occur when you listen
to your favourite music or enjoy a night out at the theatre
or cinema.

THINK ABOUT IT There is a difference between resting and
relaxation. Resting is a cessation of physical
activity for the body but does not necessarily
imply a constructive mental component to
the activity. For example, you can lie motionless on your
bed and worry. Relaxation must include the mental component which enables your mind to feel calm and at peace.
Although resting is clearly good for the body, relaxation is
more powerful since it reinvigorates body and soul.

How to relax

There are two basic routes to achieve relaxation. The first
consists of using the mind to relax the body, and the second reverses this process by using the body to relax the
mind. It is a matter of personal preference which of the two
(or combinations of the two) you elect to use. As you will

know from your own experience, when you are worrying about something, you find that your muscles become tense. Equally, when you experience physical pain or tension, it quickly impacts your mood. The mind and body influence each other closely, and the skill of relaxation uses this link to great advantage.

Techniques in which we use the mind to relax the body include *passive* muscle relaxation, guided imagery and the practices of mindfulness, hypnotherapy, meditation and autogenics. Techniques which employ the body's ability to relax the mind include *progressive* muscle relaxation, yoga, tai chi, massage and deep abdominal breathing. Some activities within these two categories overlap and involve active manipulation of both the mind and the body; for example, mindfulness and Zen meditation focus on breathing techniques as well as thought awareness. All of these techniques, or stress-busters, are vital to promote improved digestion, to lower cholesterol levels and to improve moods, to mention a fraction of their benefits. The mind and body need time to be still, nurtured and nourished. Just a few minutes of relaxation within a busy day can make all the difference to our health and well-being.

---

1. When preparing to do a relaxation exercise, check that your environment is as conducive as possible to achieving a relaxed state. Ensure that it is quiet and not too hot or

cold, dim the lighting, and choose somewhere you will not be disturbed.

2. Try to put aside a set time each day to relax. It is best if this is not straight after a heavy meal, although you should avoid starting a relaxation exercise if you are hungry or physically uncomfortable. Wear clothing in which you can relax, removing tight clothing or shoes that might inhibit the relaxation process.

3. Accept the fact that your thoughts will distract you from time to time, and do not be concerned about this; simply refocus when you become aware that you have drifted off.

4. Do not analyze your progress. The cumulative effect will eventually bear fruit. It will be easier to concentrate some days than others. Too earnest an approach is the kiss of death to relaxation. The key is not to try too hard and to allow the exercise to unfold gently.

Using the mind to relax the body
Passive muscle relaxation
This technique involves your imagination only – *not* the physical tensing and relaxing of each muscle group. (That is known as progressive muscle relaxation; see p. 133.) Just thinking about an unpleasant medical procedure or having to sit an exam can make our muscles tense; this exercise uses the same processes but in a constructive way to release

muscle tension. Simply imagining relaxing each muscle group creates a positive impact on the muscles, enabling them to relax.

This approach is very good for people who suffer from chronic pain and therefore find the actual physical tensing and relaxing of muscle groups difficult. By the same token, those suffering from heart problems and high blood pressure will find this technique more appropriate to their needs. If anyone doubts the efficacy of using imagination alone to induce physiological changes, I suggest that you picture the date of your dreams and then monitor the physical changes in your body!

Meditation and mindfulness
This section provides a brief, and therefore simplified, account of two distinct approaches. Meditative practice comes in many different forms, depending on the tradition from which it is derived: religious or secular. At its most basic level, meditation enables us to have a break from negative, destructive thoughts by focusing on something positive or neutral. It requires a defined technique, such as focusing on a mantra, symbol, word, object or breathing. During meditation, the rational or logical brain (the left hemisphere) is suspended or relaxed, becoming secondary to our creative, right-hemispheric thinking. This is a self-induced state in which we take control of our mind and elect its general direction.

In mindfulness practice, various techniques are employed

that usually involve a focus on breathing, along with an awareness of how the physical body feels. The objective of mindfulness is to develop awareness by monitoring the mind and allowing thoughts to arise and be experienced without intellectualizing or analyzing them. This enables us to conserve energy by not wasting time repelling frightening thoughts or clinging onto positive ones. Instead, we learn to accept that life is ever-changing and that no mood state endures forever, be it happiness or sadness, anger or peace. The beauty of mindfulness is that it is so versatile. By applying full concentration to any task, from washing up to gardening, brushing your teeth or eating an ice cream, you live fully in each moment. As distracting thoughts emerge you simply re-focus your attention on the task and engage all of your senses to experience the activity.

Both these techniques increase self-awareness and confidence, promote relaxation, and augment our resilience in coping with stress, along with a host of physical benefits, such as reducing blood pressure and boosting our immune system. The daily practice of these two approaches increases our energy and enables us to develop positive qualities of appreciation, generosity, patience, forgiveness and compassion, all of which make life less stressful and improve our relationships with others.

Autogenics and hypnotherapy

Autogenics is a form of self-hypnosis, whereas hypnotherapy involves hypnosis by a therapist. Both techniques make use of the brain's natural trance state, induced by imagining or suggesting that the body is warm, heavy and relaxed, and the mind calm and composed. Guided imagery is often used to enable the person to relax deeply so that they can access a highly-focused level of concentration. In this state of locked attention, the mind is receptive to exploring ideas in a positive and creative manner, and can often conceive of constructive and innovative solutions to the many problems that besiege our daily lives.

Ensure that your hypnotherapist is an appropriately trained practitioner by asking about their qualifications and whether they have regular supervision and membership of a professional body. If you elect to go down the autogenics route, seek out a bona fide course so that you can learn the techniques correctly. The autogenic training will teach you to experience sensations of heaviness, warmth and coolness, along with how to regulate your heart rate and breathing.

Guided imagery

THINK ABOUT IT

Have you ever been lost in reverie – for example, you were imagining being reunited with your lover – and had someone ask you what you are smiling about? Anticipation of an event can be so powerful, be it happy or sad, that the brain and body react in a similar way whether the event is real or imagined.

This technique is very powerful, whether used on its own or in combination with other relaxation techniques. It involves the use of all five senses, known as a polysensorial approach, along with the accompanying emotions to create a virtual experience within the mind. While it is often thought of as just trying to visualize a scene, it is so much more. When all senses are employed in guided imagery, brain imaging technology demonstrates that the brain reacts in an identical way to how it would if the person were physically present in the imagined situation.

For example, dancers often mentally rehearse in their mind their routine and accurately recreate the steps, movement, rhythm, music and attitude of the dance. In more extreme situations, starving people have soothed their hunger pangs through imagining eating a feast, and freezing people have been able to generate warmth through the use of guided imagery.

A **polysensorial** approach is one that uses our senses of touch, sight, smell, taste and sound to recreate an experience in our mind as though it were really happening.

Ask someone to read the following passage slowly, out loud. Sit or lie in a relaxed, supported position with your eyes closed, and try to incorporate all of your senses as you

130

imagine the walk described here as accurately and realistically as possible.

Guided imagery of a walk in the countryside

It is a beautiful spring morning in the southern county of Devonshire in England.

You are staying with friends in a picturesque village, very close to the coast.

You decide to take a leisurely walk along the winding country lanes to absorb the scenery and the fresh air.

The thatched cottages, tucked closely together, look cosy and inviting, and you ponder on the lives of their inhabitants.

As you pass the old rectory, you notice a fat kitten curled up peacefully on the window ledge, basking in the warmth of the morning sunshine. You too can feel the sun's rays on your exposed skin.

You stop for a moment to watch the slow rise and fall of the kitten's breathing.

The lane twists through farmland, and you gaze at the newly-born lambs as they totter and sway on the grassy slopes, acclimatizing to their new surroundings.

The quacking of a mother duck suddenly pierces the air as she marshals her brood across the lane on the way to the brook.

You look on as the ducklings, one by one, launch themselves into the water under the watchful supervision of their parent.

Your attention is then arrested by the sound of pounding hooves, as a herd of ponies chase each other from one end of the meadow to the other, tossing their heads and kicking up their legs.

The crisp morning air has given you an appetite, so you make your way to the village teashop at the far end of the lane, beside an ancient, majestic yew tree, whose canopy of yellow-grey leaves sways in the breeze.

Just before entering the shop, you can smell the aroma of freshly-baked wholemeal bread.

You decide to treat yourself to the traditional cream tea, advertised on the billboard outside.

You savour the taste of the warm scones and bread, accompanied by a selection of fine jams and thick clotted cream.

The meal is washed down with a pot of piping hot tea.

Satiated, you thank the owner, promising to return the next day to sample the homemade cakes on display.

As you amble back to your cottage, you pause to stroke an old chestnut horse, who has poked his head over the fence.

As you linger in this spot, you are conscious of your own inner peacefulness. You feel serene, totally in tune with nature.

Your breathing is slow and measured, and your entire body feels deeply relaxed.

Using the body to relax the mind

Yoga and tai chi

Yoga is an ancient Indian practice, consisting of a series of postures that are executed in coordination with breathing patterns. Yoga activates the relaxation response and decreases arousal levels, which in turn helps to soothe the mind, enabling calmness and a sense of control. You can teach yourself how to do the basic yoga poses by following the simple guidance offered on numerous websites or, better still, why not enrol in one of the classes that are available in your local area?

Tai chi is also an effective way to release stress and has many health benefits, not least the promotion of serenity and inner peace. It has been described as being like meditation in motion, although in the 13th century it was a form of martial art, the original purpose of which was defence. It is more fluid than yoga and consists of a series of gentle movements performed in slow motion, combined with deep breathing.

Progressive muscle relaxation

There are many methods of progressive muscle relaxation, all of which involve the tensing and releasing of various muscle groups in a systematic manner. Some start from the top of the head and work down to the tips of the toes, whereas others reverse the sequence. Some methods advocate holding the tension of the muscle for ten seconds and then the relaxation phase for as long as 30 seconds.

My preferred technique is to do the muscle tension in tandem with the inhalation to the count of four and then release the tension immediately on the exhalation, holding this phase for the count of four. Start with the top of the head and progress through to the temples, eyes, cheeks, jaw, neck, shoulders, arms, hands, fingers, back, chest, stomach, bottom, thighs, knees, calves, ankles, feet and toes. It should be noted that this technique is not advised for people with heart problems and high blood pressure without consulting your doctor first.

Massage

Most people are familiar with the concept of massage, a hands-on treatment in which tension is released by the application of pressure to or manipulation of muscles and joints. It is an ancient method of healing: its use is noted in 4,000-year-old medical texts. There are many different types of massage, including Thai massage, Indian head massage, remedial massage and deep abdominal massage. All of these treatments not only increase flexibility, by enabling deep layers of muscle and connective tissue to become more pliant, but also have profound relaxation benefits. As you will recall, a relaxed body facilitates a relaxed mind.

Deep abdominal breathing

When we are worried and anxious our breathing tends to become rapid and shallow, causing us to hyperventilate.

This causes the sympathetic, or arousal, branch of the autonomic nervous system to become dominant and to release stress hormones, such as cortisol, into the bloodstream. Furthermore, the decreased levels of carbon dioxide make us feel breathless and we hyperventilate all the more. Unless we slow down our rate of breathing this cycle continues and exacerbates our anxiety levels, as the distressing physical symptoms make us even more anxious.

Deep abdominal breathing, also known as diaphragmatic or belly breathing, is one of the most effective ways to induce a state of relaxation. It is particularly powerful if the exhalation is significantly longer than the inhalation, forcing the parasympathetic branch of the autonomic nervous system to become dominant. This gives the body no other choice but to relax. The vagus nerve sends a message to various organs telling them to slacken their pace while other physiological processes are resumed. As a consequence, your heart rate, blood pressure and pulse rate slow down and your digestive system operates with maximum efficiency as you move into the R & D mode (see p. 47).

See chapter 5 for step-by-step guidance on how to practise deep abdominal breathing (p. 60). Remember to start by monitoring your normal resting breathing rate; then try to make this slightly slower. Whenever you become anxious, employ this simple breathing technique to help you to relax.

7/11 breathing

The most energy-efficient and fastest way to achieve intense relaxation is to breathe in to the count of seven and out to the count of eleven.

Lie on the floor with a book placed on top of your belly button. Breathe in deeply through your nose to the count of seven, ensuring that you are pushing the air right down into your abdomen, causing your stomach to inflate. If you are doing this correctly, the book will rise up as you inhale. Then breathe out slowly through the nose to the count of eleven; as the air is exhaled the book will fall as your abdomen deflates.

This exercise works just as well whether you prefer to breathe in or out through the nose or mouth, although the smaller nasal orifices make breathing naturally slower than breathing through the larger aperture of the mouth. You might find this exercise difficult at first. If so, gradually build up your capacity by incrementally adding more to your count until you achieve 7/11 breathing.

Relaxation is an essential aspect of our nature

Whether we achieve a relaxed state through tensing and releasing our muscles, controlling our breathing, meditating or simply sitting in our garden and mindfully enjoying our surroundings, the benefits are considerable. Taking time for ourselves is not selfish since it conserves energy, enables us to offer more to others, increases self-confidence and makes us more sanguine, creative and nicer people to be around.

In a relaxed state we are more likely to daydream, a habit that has been greatly discouraged in the past but which is now coming to be recognized as a constructive activity. While daydreaming, we switch to right-hemispheric thinking, which enables us to think creatively, to spot patterns and to come up with ideas and solutions. This is why top executives often have little routine work to accomplish, leaving them sufficient time to allocate to what is known in business speak as 'blue sky thinking'.

The popular American psychologist, Dr Joyce Brothers advocated that workers should take five minutes relaxation in every hour to increase their productivity. During these restful moments of relaxation we can truly listen to ourselves, become attuned to our bodies and clear our minds. A short relaxing break yields clarity in our thinking, recharges our batteries and enables us to become mindful and centred.

Mini stress-busters

If finding a whole five minutes in every hour doesn't go down too well with your employer, try the following forms of relaxation, which take as little as 60 seconds and are known to be effective:

1. Pause for a moment and empty your mind; try to think of as little as possible.

2. Wherever you are, be it at your desk or in your car at traffic lights, take the opportunity to do a few gentle stretches of your arms, shoulders, neck and feet.

3. Periodically, stop whatever you are doing and listen to your body; scan from head to toe to discover what your body needs – for example, exercise, rest, food, liquids or sleep.

4. Tightly clench both of your fists as hard as you can and notice the whiteness of your knuckles and how the tension creeps up your arms and into your shoulders. After fifteen seconds release the tension and experience the warmth and sensation of relaxation that spreads as your fingers uncurl.

5. Listen to your mind to discover what it is craving: for example, peace, calm, energy, romance, friendship or comforting.

Although these exercises take only a minimal amount of time, you will find that when you resume your activities, you will do so with greater motivation and energy.

 If you seriously want to be able to induce the relaxation response at will, the Om-chanting technique is an excellent discipline (see p. 63). Before you start, do a quick body scan from the top of your head to your toes, ensuring that all muscle groups are relaxed (approximately one minute). For any muscles that are tense, increase the tension further and then release to experience the relaxed state. Focus on your breathing and chanting for approximately eight minutes, and then finish with a minute of relaxation as you allow your breathing to return to normal, before continuing with the rest of your day. Many of my clients find a quiet place during their lunch break and have reported that it hugely benefits their mood and efficiency throughout the afternoon.

IF YOU REMEMBER ONE THING Not to take time for rest and relaxation is a false economy, which many of us live to regret. The time that you most need to relax is when you don't have time for it! Make it a priority that you build into your day, just like allocating a set time of day for exercising.

PART THREE:
Well-being and sleep

10. What is sleep and why do we do it?

Sleep that knits up the ravell'd sleave of care,
The death of each day's life, sore labour's bath,
Balm of hurt minds, great nature's second course,
Chief nourisher in life's feast—

William Shakespeare, *Macbeth*, II.ii.34–37

Sleep plays a key role in the restoration of both the body and mind. In the same way that the brain signals hunger to compel us to eat, in a similar manner it signals tiredness to urge us to sleep. In fact, so significant is this essential component of our well-being that a human can survive three times longer without food than they can without sleep. So, the simple answer to the question of why we sleep is that it enables us to survive. But what is sleep? In brief, it is an altered state of consciousness that plays an important role in a number of essential brain and bodily functions, such as memory, learning and cell regeneration and repair, which enable healing by boosting the body's immune system.

Sleep deprivation is often the chief culprit in a number of accidents. Inadequate sleep causes more road traffic accidents than driving under the influence of alcohol, as it impairs the driver's coordination, slows reaction times and leads to poor judgement. Those operating potentially lethal machinery such as drills and chainsaws are advised of the importance of ensuring that they are fully awake when using these tools. Many prescriptions that cause drowsiness carry a health warning to this effect. Sleep deprivation has also played a crucial part in several major disasters, not least the Exxon Valdez oil spill, the Challenger Space Shuttle disaster and the Chernobyl nuclear power plant explosion.

A dozen benefits of sleep

Sleep has fascinated writers and philosophers for millennia. The ancient Roman poet Virgil described sleep as 'death's brother' and considered each nightly sleep as a mini-death. Lord Byron, a key figure in the Romantic movement of the early 19th century, also saw sleep as possessing qualities not dissimilar to death: 'Death, so call'd, is a thing that makes men weep,/ And yet a third of life is pass'd in sleep.' Even to this day death is sometimes euphemistically referred to as 'the big sleep', the term originating from Raymond Chandler's 1939 novel of the same name. We can readily understand the parallel made with death, since what can be observed by the naked eye during sleep is a huge reduction in physical activity, along with a significantly decreased degree of responsiveness to outside stimuli. Anyone who has tried to rouse a sleeping teenager will know that it often requires a concerted effort before consciousness is finally demonstrated!

However, these parallels overlook the incredibly industrious nature of the brain during sleep, and the important benefits it brings to both our physical and mental health, and hence our well-being. Sleep:

1. Improves our sense of well-being and makes us less likely to have mood swings, sadness, depression or suicidal tendencies.

2. Is crucial for growth in children and plays a key role in fertility development for teenagers.

3. Enables us to feel rested, which in turn helps us to be alert and attentive when awake and therefore prevents accidents caused by drowsiness.

4. Plays a key role in learning, as the sleeping brain forges new pathways for memory retention.

5. Enables us to make sound decisions and to be creative, more fun, highly motivated, more measured and less prone to taking risks.

6. Repairs and heals heart and blood vessels; boosts our immune system, making us better able to fight off infections; repairs cells and tissue; and strengthens bones, joints and muscles.

7. Decreases our risk of becoming obese, having a stroke, or suffering from high blood pressure, kidney disease or diabetes.

8. Is essential in facilitating a healthy hormone balance, in particular impacting ghrelin and leptin, which control hunger and insulin production and are key to maintaining correct blood sugar levels.

9. Enables us to process the day's intense emotions during the rapid eye movement (REM) sleep phase allowing us to face the following day in a calmer frame of mind.

10. Improves physical appearance (no dark circles under the eyes).

11. Keeps the body's systems synchronized to allow optimum efficiency.

12. Downshifts metabolism, thus conserving energy.

So, we know that sleep is *not* an inactive state and that it provides a range of physical and mental benefits. To understand how to achieve regular sleep, it is helpful first to look in greater detail at what goes on while we sleep.

Why do we need sleep?

As discussed, sleep is not a passive activity; it is key to our ability to function properly during the day and is a vital component of our survival. It is an altered state of consciousness and plays a significant role in a number of essential brain and bodily functions, such as memory, learning and cell regeneration and repair, which enable healing by boosting the body's immune system. Our grandmothers hit the nail on the head by advocating a good night's sleep for both physical and mental ailments.

There are a number of theories as to why we need sleep, one of which is energy conservation, brought about as a consequence of the metabolism downshifting, and thus stretching out scarce resources. Restorative theories claim that sleep provides the body with the chance to focus on repairs and regeneration. These theories have a lot of credibility, since we know that the vast majority of growth hormones are released during sleep and that deprivation of deep sleep causes the immune system to collapse.

In addition, compelling evidence from brain plasticity theory shows that sleep is essential for the development of the brain. We all know anecdotally that if we have not enjoyed a good night's sleep, we are inefficient at learning new information, since we struggle to remain focused and our attention wavers. But equally, after we have learned some new skill or knowledge we become poor learners if it is not followed by sufficient sleep. Acquisition and recall of learning clearly happen while we are awake; however, the third component of learning and memory, that is *consolidation*, happens while we sleep.

How does sleep happen?

At its simplest level, sleep is a process caused by *neurotransmitters*, which are nerve-signalling chemicals, acting on particular nerve cells known as *neurons*, which in turn switch off the signals that keep us awake or switch on those that send us to sleep. During daytime brain activity, we build up *adenosine*, a chemical that causes us to feel increasingly drowsy as it accumulates. During sleep, this chemical is broken down, thus reversing the drowsy effect as the sleep progresses.

There are two internal sleep systems, which normally work in a synchronized fashion, enabling you to be awake during the day and asleep at night. As the day progresses, one of these systems, known as your *sleep drive*, becomes more intense. However, rather than you steadily becoming sleepier as each hour passes, the second system overrides sleepiness by producing an increasing and opposite effect, known as the *circadian alerting signal*. The alerting signal has the upper hand for most of the day, but when it starts to diminish in the very late evening, the sleep drive (having been building up all day) gains supremacy and you begin to feel very sleepy. It is at the point of intersection of the accumulated sleep drive and the diminishing circadian alerting signal (at roughly 11pm), where one is able to sleep for the 'normal' eight hours.

During the night as each hour of sleep elapses, the sleep drive (which has been built up during the day) dissipates, while at the same time the alerting signal also continues to decrease. This is why we sleep most deeply during the earlier part of the night's sleep. As each hour of sleep progresses, the sleep drive diminishes and by morning time, if you have had an undisturbed sleep, it will have totally dissipated, enabling you to awake feeling refreshed and ready to start your day. Both systems then start gathering momentum again, repeating the process of build-up and dissipation every 24 hours.

Sleep drive is part of the body's homeostasis system, which maintains the correct internal environment by reacting to shortages. When we are short of food the homeostasis system will increase the hunger drive; when dehydrated it will increase the thirst drive; and when we need sleep it will increase the sleep drive. It works in tandem with the **circadian alerting signal**, which signals wakefulness and overrides the sleep drive during the day. It arises from the *suprachiasmatic nucleus* (SCN) – the internal, biological 24-hour clock, which is located in the area of the brain called the hypothalamus. The SCN controls and regulates many processes that take place every 24 hours, known as circadian rhythms.

Sleep cycle and stages

Sleep consists of a number of cycles, which last for approximately 90–110 minutes in adults who are good sleepers, thus enabling them to complete an average of five cycles per night.

During a person's lifetime sleep cycles change. The average infant sleeps far longer than the average adult norm of eight hours, and adults over the age of 50 years frequently sleep far less. In addition, the proportion of REM sleep declines with age, and variations in the quantity of deep sleep can be very marked too. Everyone will have their own unique sleep pattern, there is no one size that fits all when it comes to how much sleep we need.

 Ask your family and friends how many hours they currently sleep and whether they have noticed a change in their sleep pattern over their lifetime. Can you detect any patterns between the groups? How much do sleeping habits vary from one person to the next? Does the information help to shed any light on your own sleeping habits?

A full sleep cycle includes four distinct phases, which repeat and alternate throughout the sleep:

1. Rapid eye movement (REM) sleep

2. Stage One Non-rapid eye movement (NREM) sleep

3. Stage Two Non-rapid eye movement (NREM) sleep

4. Stage Three Non-rapid eye movement (NREM) sleep

Rapid eye movement (REM) sleep
During REM sleep, which makes up about 25 per cent of your sleeping time, you do most of your dreaming. Your blood pressure, heart rate and breathing fluctuate during this sleep, and you might also experience slight twitching. It is the most active stage for your brain and body functions.

It is called rapid eye movement sleep since, as the name suggests, your eyes move rapidly and your major muscles become paralyzed to prevent you from acting out your dreams. In adult sleeping patterns it is usually the last part of the sleep cycle. It is very brief in the first cycle, lasting just a couple of minutes, but becomes progressively longer as you complete each cycle, resulting in the REM sleep being approximately 30 minutes in the final cycle just before you wake up.

Non-rapid eye movement (NREM) sleep

NREM sleep makes up 75 per cent of nightly sleep in adults and 50 per cent in babies (who spend the other 50 per cent in the REM phase). This type of sleep is less active than REM and is characterized by diminished neural activity. NREM is divided into three stages:

- **Stage one** – This phase is the briefest of the NREM sleep phases and is the start of the cycle when you first fall asleep. It is a transitional stage from wakefulness to a very light sleep from which you can be easily aroused. You will only revisit this stage if you are disturbed and wake up in the night – though you might not always be aware that you have done so. If you think of the average sleep cycle lasting 100 minutes, you will spend roughly five minutes in this stage. The features of this sleep are slow, rolling movements of the eyes and the start of muscle relaxation. Your brainwaves will change from the *beta* waves of wakefulness to the *alpha* waves of relaxation to the *theta* waves of light sleep.

- **Stage two** – This phase is the largest portion of the average 100-minute cycle and makes up 50 per cent of total sleep in adults. Your eyes will become stationary and your muscles will be even more deeply relaxed. The brain still produces the *theta* waves of light sleep, along with *sleep spindles*, which are bursts of rapid rhythmic brainwaves, and *K-complexes*, which are brainwaves believed to be part of memory development that also reduce alertness to external stimuli. Your heart rate slows down and your body temperature will start to drop as this stage progresses. During this stage it is considerably harder to wake a person than during the first stage of NREM as the sleeper becomes increasingly unaware of external stimuli. This stage appears more frequently in the sleep pattern since it both precedes and follows stage three and REM sleep during the sleep sequence. The cycles will continue in this manner unless the sleeper wakes up, in which case stage one will be repeated. Sleeping medication may also disrupt the natural sequence of the cycles.

- **Stage three** – This phase is the deepest sleep of all and is longer in the early sleep cycles. It accounts for 20 per cent of sleep when averaged out throughout the night. It decreases considerably in the later sleep cycles, tailing off into almost non-existence in the final cycle. In children this sleep stage is more prominent both in duration and depth, which accounts for why it is so difficult to rouse a child from this stage. This explains how toddlers can remain sound asleep in their parent's arms even when they are running for a bus. Some elderly adults do not achieve stage three NREM at all and become much lighter sleepers. During this stage the muscles are most deeply relaxed and *delta waves* occur in the brain, which render you unconscious and allow the body to heal. If you are roused from sleep during this stage you are most likely to suffer from *sleep inertia*: the feeling of grogginess that we sometimes experience when we first wake up and find it hard to think straight or coordinate our limbs.

Brainwaves refer to the electrical activity caused by the communication between millions of your brain cells (known as neurons) via neurotransmitters. Each type of brainwave pattern denotes a particular mental state, for example: awake or in the REM phase.

Gamma waves are required for learning, memory processing, language development and the formation of ideas.

Beta waves are present when a person is wide awake and are involved in conscious thought and focus.

Alpha waves are present when you close your eyes and are very relaxed but still awake (a state often achieved through meditation). Alpha waves enable the individual to experience pain to a lesser degree as well as reducing anxiety. They signal the transition from wakefulness to the beginning of falling asleep.

Theta waves are present in extreme relaxation, light sleep (Stage One NREM) and the state used in hypnotherapy. During this state the brain is very receptive to new ideas and suggestions. Theta waves are also present in Stage Two NREM, accompanied by sleep spindles and K-complexes.

Delta waves are the slowest brainwaves of all, which render you unconscious, as in Stage Three NREM sleep (which is also known as slow wave recuperative sleep). This state is when your body heals itself, resets your internal clocks and boosts your immune system.

Sleep spindles (also known as sigma waves) occur during Stage Two NREM sleep and consist of clusters of small, rapid waves, which enable the brain to consolidate new learning with established learning.

K-complexes are large waves that appear during Stage Two NREM sleep and are believed to play a part in memory development, as well as causing the sleeper to become less alert to external stimuli.

A 'typical' adult sleep cycle (repeated approximately five times during one period of sleep)

Stage 1 NREM	Light sleep as you transition from awake to asleep, characterized by relaxation. Occurs only in the first cycle unless you wake up in the night.
Stage 2 NREM	Deeper muscle relaxation as your heart rate slows and body temperature drops.
Stage 3 NREM	Deepest sleep in which your body recuperates. May not occur in older adults or during the later cycles.
Stage 2 NREM	
REM	An active sleep state in which you dream, your heart rate and temperature fluctuate and your major muscles become paralyzed.
Stage 2 NREM	
Stage 3 NREM	

Having now understood what sleep consists of and the benefits it affords, it is important to learn how we can reap those benefits to the maximum by improving the quality of our sleep.

How much sleep do we need?

This is a most vexatious question, which has teased mankind for ages. Why do some people need more sleep than others? Why do babies sleep significantly longer than the elderly? Why do some animals require minimal hours of sleep? Does the quantity of sleep equate to the complexity of the brain? Does the amount of sleep needed depend on whether you are prey or predator? And so the questions around quantity of sleep abound.

So far we have talked about what a 'normal', or typical, sleep looks like (90–110-minute cycles, with an average of five cycles per sleep). However, this norm simply represents an average, not a benchmark that your individual sleeping pattern will or should follow. We will touch more on the variations in sleep patterns in chapter 11 when we examine ways to improve our sleep habits, but the important thing to remember is that quality of sleep matters more than quantity. Quality sleep makes a fundamental difference in determining our resilience to withstanding mental and physical ill health.

11. Practical advice to improve sleep

The unappealing term 'sleep hygiene' has wormed its way into most of the literature relating to sleeping habits. Don't worry, it has nothing to do with how frequently you change your bed sheets or whether or not you take a shower before going to bed! Instead, it refers to the development of constructive habits to improve your sleep pattern.

What I will refer to as the *facilitate sleep regimen* (FSR) is another way of addressing your lifestyle in an ordered manner to provide a conducive foundation for regular, quality sleep. The *smart bedtime routine* (SBR) relates to both the organization of your physical environment and the implementation of helpful pre-sleep practices. For the purpose of the advice and tips that follow, I am making the assumption that you intend to take all of your sleep requirements in one session at night, since humans are by nature *diurnal monophasic* creatures, that is, they are active during the day and prefer to sleep in one prolonged session over the course of a 24-hour period. However, this may not always be possible if you regularly take long-haul flights or do shift work, which disrupt the natural sleep patterns.

KEY TERMS

Diurnal refers to being active during the day, in contrast to *nocturnal* which refers to animals that are active at night.

Monophasic sleep refers to one prolonged session of sleep over the course of 24 hours. This contrasts with *polyphasic sleep*, preferred by the majority of animals, which refers to sleeping in multiple sessions over the course of 24 hours.

THINK ABOUT IT

In some countries a polyphasic sleep pattern is often practised in the form of a prolonged afternoon nap (of up to two hours), known as a siesta. Several countries in the Mediterranean and Latin America engage in this practice. It is seen as the perfect foil to the intense afternoon heat in tropical and sub-tropical climates, which can hinder concentration and cause a slump in productivity. The siesta also provides favourable conditions in which to cope with the drowsy effects of a heavy midday meal, affording the perfect opportunity to rest and digest. As global warming progresses it could be a cultural idiosyncrasy that many other countries would do well to adopt. Patagonia already indulges in an afternoon sleep without having a hot climate as an excuse. However, the likelihood of this catching on more broadly is hampered by the logistics of many modern businesses, which, of course, usually put commerce before health!

Variations

It should be noted that the idea of a single sleep is an 'ideal', or 'pure', type that refers to generalized behaviour. As we well know, some people feel more active in the morning and are often referred to as 'larks', after the early-rising song-bird, while others are more productive and lively at the end of the day and are known as 'night owls', after the mostly nocturnal bird of prey. There is, of course, every variance in between, and each individual will have their own unique pattern of peaks and troughs in alertness and inactivity.

Facilitate sleep regimen (FSR)

In order to optimize your chances of achieving quality sleep it is important to adjust aspects of your lifestyle. I am not suggesting that this is a regimen to which you should slavishly adhere since, inevitably, the impact of travelling, attending celebratory occasions and so forth will cause you to digress from time to time. However, from a long-term perspective, try to incorporate the following practices into your everyday way of life.

Reduce stimulants

Regulate your use of stimulants throughout the day. Nicotine, caffeine and many recreational drugs are powerful stimulants and prevent sleep. Despite people saying that smoking a cigarette or other tobacco-based products relaxes them, it actually stimulates the central nervous system. Try to avoid smoking in the evening and definitely do not reach for a cigarette if you find it hard to get to sleep at night.

Caffeine, found in many soft drinks, like cola or soda, in pain medication, chocolate, tea and coffee are a definite no just before bedtime. In fact, you would be well advised to avoid anything containing caffeine from about five hours before you plan to sleep. You may find it useful to switch to decaffeinated drinks and herbal teas, which are readily available. It is best to cut down your caffeine consumption gradually if you wish to avoid withdrawal symptoms. Do not be surprised if you initially suffer from headaches if you are a heavy caffeine consumer when you start to limit your daily intake.

Monitor food and drink intake

The old maxim of 'breakfast like a king, lunch like a prince and dine like a pauper' is sound advice for getting a good night's sleep, along with allowing at least three hours of digestion time before trying to sleep. Going to bed shortly after a substantial meal is asking for trouble since this is likely to make you feel uncomfortably full or bloated, which makes falling asleep difficult. Once asleep you will also be more prone to sleep disturbance from digestive upsets. This is because lying down makes problems like acid reflux more likely, since you do not have the benefit of gravity to prevent its occurrence. Try to avoid foods that cause indigestion such as fatty or spicy foods as this will impede your ability to get to sleep in a timely manner.

Some deficiencies in your diet can lead to sleep issues,

so consider making changes to your diet in addition to behavioural changes to improve sleep. For instance, tryptophan is an important building block of protein that is not produced by the body, but must be obtained from food or dietary supplements. The body uses tryptophan to make niacin, a B vitamin that not only aids digestion but also plays a key role in serotonin production. Serotonin is a chemical that affects our mood and enables us to feel relaxed and comfortable, which in turn aids sleep. Tryptophan is found in great abundance in sea lions, which are unlikely to be readily available in your local supermarket, unless you are living in Alaska! However, other rich sources of this essential amino acid can be found in game, poultry (especially turkey), egg whites, milk, dates, cottage cheese, cod, salmon, bananas, soybeans and seeds, such as sesame and sunflower.

Magnesium deficiency is related to insomnia, so it might be helpful to check this out with your doctor if you have been having trouble getting to sleep. There are various magnesium supplements on the market, along with sprays that you can use on your skin to aid sleep; these should only be purchased from reputable sources and under medical guidance. Additionally, magnesium can be found in almonds, pumpkin seeds and spinach. A deficiency of potassium, an essential mineral salt, has been linked to difficulties in remaining asleep due to being woken up by cramp. Potassium tends to work synergistically with magnesium and both can be derived from avocados and Swiss chard. It is always preferable to obtain these necessary minerals from your diet whenever possible. Other good sources of potassium are Brussels sprouts, Romaine lettuce, broccoli and celery.

Endeavour to drink plenty of water throughout the day since this not only prevents dehydration but also aids digestion. However, as with eating, do not drink a large amount just before going to bed, as this will result in your needing to get up in the middle of the night and can prove very disruptive to your sleep pattern. Finally, remember that feeling hungry before going to bed can cause wakefulness just as much as feeling overly stuffed. If you are feeling peckish, try to make do with a very light snack, preferably made up of dairy and carbohydrates, which should settle the hunger pangs and enable you to feel satisfied. Dairy products containing tryptophan have been shown to have a calming effect. The tryptophan, as discussed earlier, is converted to an amino acid called L-tryptophan, which is responsible for the production of relaxing neurotransmitters such as serotonin and melatonin. Carbohydrates cause the release of insulin, which helps to clear away from the blood stream other types of amino acids that compete with L-tryptophan, thus enabling the brain to manufacture more serotonin and melatonin. (For further discussion of the relaxing properties of tryptophan, see p. 112)

Be aware of the impact of alcohol
Alcohol deserves a special mention since it is rather confusing in that it is a depressant and therefore should aid sleep.

Like any hypnotic drug it does help you to get to sleep initially but it changes your correct sleeping pattern. Instead of having your usual quota of five or six REM sleep cycles you will be reduced to just a few and will be prevented from enjoying the benefits of deep sleep. This is because as the alcohol metabolizes and is gradually absorbed into the body you may experience mild withdrawal symptoms, which will rouse you. Combined with the fact that you are likely to also feel dehydrated, you will wake up from your light sleep feeling tired rather than refreshed.

Since alcohol is a diuretic, it will not only cause you to sweat throughout the night to get rid of fluids but will also lead to extra visits to the bathroom. If you really have overdone the alcohol consumption and have woken up with a hangover, the best remedy is none other than a bacon sandwich. The combination of carbohydrates (bread) – a source of energy – and protein (bacon) – which will break down into amino acids – will go some way towards clearing your head and restoring your depleted neurotransmitters.

Finally, if this doesn't convince you that over-consuming alcohol is a bad idea for your sleep, then consider this further incentive. Drinking alcohol before bedtime relaxes the muscles in your nose, mouth and throat, thus obstructing the smooth airflow and causing a nasty vibration – very loud snoring. This might not bother you if you are out for the count, but if you have a sleeping companion, they are unlikely to be best pleased. As the saying goes: 'When you laugh the whole world laughs with you, but when you snore you sleep alone'. To summarize, if you want an alcoholic beverage with your evening meal, then ensure that you allow at least one hour of processing time per unit before hitting the sack if you don't want a fitful night's sleep.

Exercise regularly

Exercise helps to ensure that we remain physically fit, which in turn enhances our chances of enjoying undisturbed sleep (see chapter 7). Exercising is extremely important in helping us to keep to a healthy weight, which aids sleep by reducing tho chances of developing sleep disorders linked to excess weight such as sleep apnoea. If you are trying to lose excess weight, it must be done gradually, since rapid, significant weight loss is extremely disruptive to sleep patterns, largely due to the ensuing mood swings that result from your body not receiving the necessary nutrients it needs to function properly.

The time of day in which we exercise is critical in relation to sleep quality. Exercise should not be done just before going to bed since it stimulates the nervous system, producing the hormone cortisol, which makes us feel alert. However, regular daily exercising – preferably completed at least three hours before going to bed – is excellent for promoting a good night's sleep. Outdoor exercise is very beneficial, since it enables you to increase your vitamin D levels through exposure of the skin to sunlight. Vitamin D deficiency is linked to excessive daytime sleepiness. As always, a sensible balance must be struck between adequate exposure to sunlight and protection of the skin from harmful UV rays. Remember that the sun is not your only source of vitamin D; it can also be taken as a supplement and is added to various foods, such as yogurt and cereals.

Include relaxation in your daily routine

People with hectic lifestyles claim that they are too busy to relax and yet they are the very people that need it the most. Don't be short-sighted about this most valuable daily addition to your regimen, as being relaxed can be a great help in preparing you for sleep. Additionally, you may find some of the relaxation techniques useful in getting you to sleep, as they allow you to let go of the worries and thoughts of the day (see chapter 9 for more on relaxation).

Smart bedtime routine (SBR)

Environment

Ensure that your sleeping environment is conducive to sleep. The following ideas may help you to create a sleep sanctuary:

1. **Noise** – The quieter your bedroom is, the better. If you are kept awake by chirping birds, noisy traffic or loud neighbours, use earplugs or invest in a white noise machine. Evict snoring partners or have them seek help for their problem, and remove loudly ticking clocks. If you must have your dog or cat in the bedroom at night, remove any jangling dog tags or bells, so you are not disturbed if your pet moves around.

2. **Darkness** – Light inhibits sleep, since, as diurnal creatures, it is our cue to be up and active. So as not to
   disrupt your body's production of melatonin, a hormone
   that is produced only in darkness and that affects the
   circadian rhythm, use blackout shades or heavy curtains
   to block out light. An eye mask may also be a useful
   addition to your bedtime paraphernalia.

3. **Bed** – Ensure that your bed is comfortable and that the
   mattress has not given up the ghost (they usually last
   for ten years). Regular rotation of the mattress as well as
   turning it over can help to prolong its life, but not indefi-
   nitely! Take time to find the right degree of firmness in
   both your mattress and pillows, and learn to recognize
   and avoid any material or detergent you are allergic to.

4. **Temperature** – The ambient temperature of the room
   depends on your personal preference, but should be
   between 15 and 24° Celsius (60–75° Fahrenheit). The
   temperature of your feet is surprisingly sensitive and has
   a great influence on your ability to sleep. So, if your feet
   are feeling too cold to sleep, make sure to keep them
   warm with bed socks, or if you're feeling too hot, keep
   them uncovered.

5. **Ventilation** – It is important that your room is well ven-
   tilated, since stuffy air is not conducive to sound sleep.
   Even in the depths of winter, try to leave your window
   open, even just a crack, since it will make a significant

difference to the air quality, particularly if your bedroom is small.

Melatonin, a derivative of serotonin, is a hormone that plays a key role in the modulation of sleep patterns by impacting the circadian rhythm, which is affected by light and temperature and regulates when you should sleep.

Establish a winding down routine

Make sure that you draw a proper close to the working day by ensuring that any urgent matters are concluded several hours before planning to go to sleep. Any outstanding concerns that arise should be put on a list to be tackled the next day. Instead, use your evening to enjoy yourself and wind down: have a relaxing dinner, enjoy a leisure pursuit, such as watching TV, reading a book or engaging in a favourite hobby.

Later in the evening, many people find it helpful to do a short meditation, followed by a bath to help them to relax. You may find that using bubble bath solution, essential oils or Epsom salts in the bath and surrounding yourself with scented candles adds to the relaxation experience.

Just before going to bed, do not engage in deep meaningful, emotional discussions or explore work-related problems, as this will only defeat the state of drowsiness you have cultivated with the previous activities. Make yourself a warm, milky drink or a cup of chamomile tea and honey before retiring to bed and have a glass of water by your bedside should you become thirsty during the night. Resist attempting to sleep until you actually feel sleepy, as this will just lead to frustration if you don't nod off rapidly. As far as is practicable, however, try to go to bed at a regular time each night and get up at the same time each morning, since this helps to get your body into a routine. Even though it is tempting to have a lie-in at the weekend or on holiday, it does disturb your sleep pattern.

Once you have gone to bed and turned off the light, if you don't drift off reasonably swiftly, you might like to engage in a progressive muscle relaxation exercise (see p. 133) or guided visualization (see p. 129) or the paradoxical intention technique. If none of these techniques works within fifteen minutes, get up and go to another room to pursue a relaxing task like listening to music or reading until you do feel sleepy; then return to bed at this point. This process is known as stimulus control.

KEY TERMS

Paradoxical intention technique is where you try to stay awake, which prevents you from trying too hard to fall asleep. It is akin to the idea of trying *not* to think about pink elephants, which usually does the exact opposite.

Stimulus control refers to building up an association between bed and sleep, so that when you go to bed, you're primed for sleep. Another aspect of stimulus control is electing how much time you actually spend in bed.

Do not be a clock-watcher and, if necessary, turn the clock face away from you so that you can't wind yourself up with anxiety-provoking thoughts such as 'I should be asleep by now. If I don't get to sleep soon I will feel dreadful tomorrow'. The body can cope with a few nights of poor rest, so just try to be sanguine about it and don't exacerbate the situation by worrying. A sleep deficit will increase your sleep drive, which will increase the likelihood of you sleeping soundly the following night.

Try to be relaxed and philosophical if sleep eludes you; it is crucial that you do not become irritated or upset, as this will result in the release of a cocktail of stress hormones into your body. This will make you even more alert and will further diminish the prospect of achieving a sound night's sleep. Furthermore, if you do have to get out of bed because you can't sleep, try to use the minimum amount of light possible since light is a catalyst which tells your internal clock that it is time to be awake.

 This evening, review your day and first jot down any outstanding concerns or issues that you need to attend to tomorrow. Next, consider tomorrow's events and priorities, and add these to your list. Having compiled your list and made your preparations to attend to these matters the next day, give yourself permission to put them aside. Keep your list by your bedside and, should you wake up with a nagging thought, add it to your list. You can then be disciplined about letting go of the thought, confident in the knowledge that you have recorded it and will address it the following day.

Use your bedroom exclusively for sleep and sex

TVs, computers, smartphones and all other gadgets should be banished from the bedroom. Don't have a landline phone in the bedroom, and try to avoid bringing in any work-related activities, as these destroy the association made by your brain that diving under the covers equates to sleep or fun. After all, it is about conditioning your brain and establishing a habit. In addition, most of these gadgets emit light, which suppresses melatonin production and disrupts your ability to sleep. This provides another good reason to remove them from the bedroom.

You may allow some exceptions to this rule, for example, bringing a relaxing book into your room if this helps you to unwind before settling down to sleep (horror and on-the-edge-of-your-mattress thrillers should be avoided). Similarly, if listening to a favourite piece of mellow music floats your boat, this too is appropriate. Many people find that playing CDs that are purposely designed to help you drift off to sleep can prove to be quite effective.

TRY IT NOW!

Soaking in a bath containing Epsom salts for at least twenty minutes not only improves your skin but also helps you to relax. Two cups of this natural mineral compound, consisting of magnesium and sulphate, if added to your bath water, will be absorbed by your skin and help you to de-stress. There are some conditions for which a salt bath may not be advised, such as being dehydrated or pregnant, or suffering from cardiovascular problems, burns or open wounds. So do check with your doctor if you are uncertain about the appropriateness of this therapy.

Try an aromatherapy bath using an oil that promotes relaxation, such as: ylang ylang, sandalwood, juniper, clary sage, chamomile, frankincense, rosewood, basil or bergamot. If you suffer from insomnia, lavender and marjoram are the top oils to choose. You can also spray lavender on your pillow at night or use lavender soap and cream to encourage drowsiness.

Dealing with tiredness during the day

During the daytime, endeavour to get as much natural light as you can to help you to stay awake and alert. A short walk during your lunch break will not only provide you with an opportunity to engage in beneficial exercise, but the sun light will also energize you and make you less prone to suffering from the post-lunch slump, also known as *afternoon apathy syndrome* (AAS). If you still struggle with tiredness, napping may prove beneficial.

Napping

Even a short nap can yield immediate benefits. Many great artists, inventors and statesmen believed it to be essential, not only for rest but as a means of unlocking their creativity. Luminaries like Salvador Dali, Thomas Edison, Albert Einstein, Lyndon B. Johnson and Napoleon Bonaparte made napping part of their daily routine. Winston Churchill wrote of his habit:

> Nature has not intended mankind to work from eight in the morning until midnight without that refreshment of blessed oblivion which, even if it only lasts twenty minutes, is sufficient to renew all the vital forces.[1]

The power nap, a term coined by James Maas and previously referred to as a 'catnap', is worthy of special mention. For those people who have no problem in achieving sleep given sufficient opportunity, the power nap is extremely useful and efficacious. However, for those who suffer from insomnia it should be avoided at all costs; if this is not possible, napping should never occur after 5pm since it will actively contribute towards maintaining insomnia. For

---

[1] Reproduced with permission of Curtis Brown, London on behalf of the Estate of Sir Winston Churchill. Copyright © Winston S. Churchill.

people with insomnia, taking a nap causes 'sleep-napping' in that it steals from bedtime sleep (in the same way that kid*napping* involves the snatching of people). A nap should optimally last between 10–30 minutes. Experiments have shown that an under 10-minute nap does not improve alertness and mental performance; if prolonged beyond 30 minutes, the sleeper risks going into sleep inertia, which causes disorientation and grogginess, thus making the person worse off than they were before the nap.

A **power nap** is sleep of a short duration that ends before the sleeper enters the deep sleep phase and serves to reinvigorate and refresh a person.

Tiredness on the road

As those of us who have attended boring lectures know to our cost, should we be spotted by the lecturer, it is perfectly possible to nod off while sitting upright in a chair! Many of us will have also experienced that terrifying sensation while driving on the motorway of the sudden, irresistible urge to sleep. The tell-tale signs are all too familiar: excessive blinking, heavy eyelids, straining to focus, frequent yawning, head drooping, drifting from one lane to the next and even hitting the hard shoulder, along with difficulty in recalling where you should exit. These signs should be heeded as soon as possible to avoid an accident. It is not enough to let in fresh air to jolt you into a state of wakefulness. You must stop and take a break at the earliest and safest opportunity. Studies have shown that driving accidents caused by tiredness are radically decreased if a cup of coffee is consumed, followed immediately by a 15-minute nap. The caffeine will take up to 30 minutes to take effect so will not prevent you from sleeping.

12. Sleep problems and treatments

You may find that following the practical ideas discussed in the last chapter enables you to achieve a good quality of sleep. However, if you suffer from a more serious sleep disorder, you may benefit from medical intervention. Many people suffer the odd night or two of poor sleep, and this usually will right itself naturally. However, 70 million people in the USA suffer from some form of sleep disorder. In the UK, the Mental Health Foundation estimates that nearly one third of the population suffer from insomnia to varying degrees. Seeking help from your doctor is important if you suffer from poor quality sleep, since the long-term effects of sleep deprivation can take a toll on your well-being. This chapter will help you to recognize whether you need to take further steps to improve your sleep.

Sleep disorders

There are over a hundred different types of sleep disorders, which cause individuals varying degrees of difficulty. Here are brief descriptions of the most common disorders that people encounter.

Insomnia includes problems with falling asleep or staying asleep, leading to not being able to achieve sufficient hours of sleep and consequently feeling unrested.

There are a variety of *circadian disorders*, including the advanced sleep phase, which results in an inability to delay sleep until a normal bedtime, going to sleep early in the evening but then waking up in the middle of the night. Delayed sleep phase involves going to bed in the early hours of the morning, having been unable to initiate sleep earlier and then not being able to get up in time for school or work.

Narcolepsy consists of many different symptoms, including sleep attack (an uncontrollable urge to fall asleep in the daytime), sleep paralysis (the inability to move voluntarily), cataplexy (sudden loss of muscle tone) and hypnagogic or hypnopompic hallucinations (dreamlike visions when falling asleep or waking up).

Hypersomnia is characterized by excessive sleepiness leading to extended sleeping.

Parasomnias refer to sleepwalking, night terrors, nightmares, sleep talking, bruxism (teeth-grinding), REM behaviour disorder (muscle tone is retained during the REM phase, enabling dream enactment, which can often be violent) and confusional arousals (very confused after waking up).

Restless legs syndrome involves the irresistible urge to move one's leg(s) causing the sleeper to wake up. Similarly, periodic limb movement disorder involves making involuntary jerky limb movements, causing disruption of sleep, which leads to sleepiness in the day.

Central sleep apnoea is caused by breathing pauses

that result from physical obstructions to the airways, usually accompanied by loud snoring; these cause brief awakenings and lead to excessive daytime sleepiness.

Gastroesophageal reflux is the regurgitation of stomach contents, or heartburn, causing disruption of sleep.

Many sleep disorders can lead to morning headaches, impaired mental functioning and moodiness, as well as daytime sleepiness. Low energy levels compromise people's capacity to apply themselves to their work, and exhaustion can lead to absenteeism and depression. More worryingly, tiredness can lead to injuries for people operating dangerous machinery, performing manual jobs or driving. Sleep medicine has made considerable advances in recent years, and these conditions can be treated, so don't put off seeking help if you identify with any of these conditions.

Treatments

Medication

It is widely accepted that medication is seldom a long-term answer to sleep problems. The body merely develops a tolerance as the concentration level of the drug builds up in the bloodstream, and dosages have to be increased in order to derive the same benefits. Doctors, therefore, are naturally concerned about some types of sleep medication's potential for dependency or addiction, along with concerns about the risk of undesirable side effects.

However, there is a place for medication use in the short term for re-establishing sleep patterns and dealing with sleep deprivation, particularly an inability to sleep resulting from severe trauma. Your GP will help you to weigh up the pros and cons when deciding if medication is the way forward, since lack of sleep not only prevents daytime functioning but can also lead to anxiety and depression, as well as a raft of physical symptoms, such as tension headaches, stomach upsets and, of course, a depleted immune system.

In some countries, like the USA, melatonin supplements can be bought over the counter without a prescription. In the UK, the NHS strongly recommends that it is only suitable for people who are 55 years and over. Medical supervision is advised for those considering taking melatonin since there are a number of conditions for which it is not advised, including allergies, or liver, kidney or autoimmune problems.

Questions about medication

If the possibility of medication is under discussion, it is important to ask your medical practitioner the following questions:

1. Is a pharmacological approach to my sleeping problem the only option and, if not, what else is available?

2. Can I use a combination of medication and other therapies?

3. What medication do you recommend and why?

4. What are the side effects of the various options, and which drugs should I definitely avoid if I am pregnant or have kidney, liver or heart problems?

5. What should I do if I suffer from any side effects? Should any in particular be of more concern and require me to seek immediate medical attention rather than just to discontinue the medication and make a further appointment to see you to consider other options?

6. What time of day should I take the medication, and should I take it with or without food?

7. How long will the medication you are proposing remain in my system, and will I need to change any aspects of my routine as a result?

8. For how long do you suggest that I take the medication, or how will I know that I no longer need to continue?

9. What other things might impact the drug's efficacy? Should I avoid consuming alcohol or other kinds of food or drink, or taking cold remedies or other medication?

10. What other options do I have if the medication does not agree with me or appears to not be helping me with my problem?

11. Can I stop taking the medication suddenly? If not, how long will it take me to complete a planned withdrawal schedule under your guidance, and what are the potential withdrawal symptoms I may experience?

12. How frequently will I need to make appointments with you to monitor the withdrawal process?

13. If I decide to take sleeping medication, do you recommend that I measure and adjust the dosage to only take the minimum required to yield sufficient benefits, or should I stick rigidly to the dose you prescribe?

14. Do you suggest that I alternate between two different types of drug to lower the potential for dependency?

15. Is there any other question that you would ask if you were in my shoes?

Sleep clinics

There are various treatments on offer for the numerous sleep disorders that you can research or explore with your doctor. One of the key treatments you might discuss with your doctor is the possibility of being referred to a sleep clinic. Many people are anxious about what a visit to a sleep clinic entails. So, to dispel some of the myths, here is a brief summary of what is involved.

A sleep clinic will offer you several different tests depending upon your symptoms. A *polysomnogram* (PSG) forms the basic test and electronically monitors your activities while you sleep; it usually requires a single overnight stay at the clinic. The PSG is fairly comprehensive and includes a range of measurements, such as levels of oxygen in the blood, breathing patterns, heart rhythms and limb movements.

Specific tests may be conducted to measure brainwaves, muscle tonality and eye movement (*electroencephalography* (EEG), *electromyography* (EMG), and *electrooculography* (EOG), respectively). These transmissions are recorded and then analysed by a sleep specialist, to determine if you have a disorder and, if so, which one.

Further tests are available and are geared towards suspected disorders, such as narcolepsy or sleep apnoea. This can involve a longer stay in the clinic, such as a 24-hour or two-night stay. In addition, you may find that a nasal airflow sensor and a snore microphone are used to record airflow if *obstructive sleep apnoea* (OSA) is being considered.

These tests are not invasive and merely involve the application of surface electrodes on your scalp and face. A probe, known as an oximeter, will be placed on one finger, and a series of belts will be put on your abdomen and chest.

Possible treatments
Depending on what the results reveal, you will be advised on treatment. If you have a circadian disorder, the treatment suggested might be *bright light therapy* (BLT) – not to be mistaken for a bacon, lettuce and tomato sandwich, which

goes by the same abbreviation. For those with obstructive sleep apnoea, *positional therapy* may be recommended, which basically prevents you from sleeping on your back and thus facilitates the opening of airways. Alternatively, oral appliances or *continuous positive airway pressure* (CPAP), which involve wearing a mouth guard or special mask during sleep, may be recommended. There are a wide variety of treatments available for insomnia, and since this disorder afflicts so many people, the next chapter looks at it in detail.

13. Insomnia

The term insomnia is derived from the Latin word *insomnis*, meaning sleepless. It is usually defined as difficulty falling or staying asleep for a sufficient length of time to feel rested. Symptoms include:

- Poor quality sleep

- Difficulty in falling asleep

- Difficulty in staying asleep

- Waking up too early or being totally dependent on an alarm clock to wake up

- Feeling tired and sleepy

- Needing frequent cups of coffee or other stimulants to stay awake

- Feeling irritable, depressed, anxious or having other mood swings

- Experiencing problems with memory, concentration and learning

- Lack of motivation and low energy levels, leading to poor performance

- Worried about lack of sleeping

- Tension headaches and stomach upsets

- Frequent ill health due to a depleted immune system.

Insomnia can be acute or chronic

Insomnia is referred to as *acute* (that is short-term) if it lasts for a few days to a few weeks. Usually acute insomnia can be traced readily to stresses such as working too hard or worrying about family problems, too much excitement or physical exercise just before going to bed or even napping during the day. By and large, acute insomnia corrects itself once harmony is restored in your life, particularly if you follow the facilitate sleep regimen (FSR) and the smart bedtime routine (SBR) (see pp. 159, 165).

If insomnia persists for months and years it is described as *chronic*, since it is long-term. In these cases, it usually requires some sort of intervention to correct the disorder. Chronic insomnia is further divided into *primary*, a distinct sleeping problem where the cause is little understood (although serious trauma can cause long-term insomnia), or *secondary*, where sleeplessness is a side effect of other sleep disorders, medical conditions, mental health disorders, medications or substances.

Visit your doctor

Inability to achieve regular, quality sleep can blight your life and enormously impact your sense of well-being. If you have been suffering from insomnia for two or three weeks and, despite implementing FSR and SBR, the situation is not improving and the lack of sleep is affecting your ability to function, visit your GP.

Your doctor will most likely ask you to describe your sleep patterns and lifestyle, so keeping a sleep diary will be most helpful. Once your doctor has ruled out other clinical possibilities, for example, depression or mineral or vitamin deficiencies (such as lack of iron, calcium, vitamins A or B12 and niacin, which all aid sleep), then medication or other options might be considered. It is also possible that you may be referred to a sleep clinic (see chapter 12).

Insomnia treatment options

For sufferers of insomnia, it may be suggested that you use *biofeedback*, which is a therapy that uses sound cues or images to enable you to control mental activity and muscle tension, or multicomponent therapy, which as the name implies consists of a combination of treatments. By far the most prescribed form of treatment, which also achieves the highest success rates, is a form of cognitive behavioural therapy specifically designed for insomnia, referred to as *CBT-I* (the 'I' denoting insomnia). One of the reasons for the high success rate of this treatment is the specialized training CBT-I practitioners must undergo. Before embarking on this treatment, ensure that your therapist is not just a generic CBT practitioner but has received the specific training for insomnia.

Cognitive behavioural therapy for insomnia (CBT-I)

CASE STUDY

Agatha had suffered from poor sleep for several years, which was exacerbated when her sister Stella fell when alighting from a bus, rendering her wheelchair-bound. Agatha found that the added stress involved in being Stella's primary carer further aggravated her inability to fall asleep at night. Due to her increasing exhaustion, Agatha tried to make up for her sleep deprivation by going to bed progressively earlier, but the situation only continued to deteriorate. The physiotherapist, who visited Stella for her daily exercises, noticed Agatha's escalating tiredness and enquired if she was sleeping properly.

As a result of their discussion, Agatha went to see her doctor who ran some tests to exclude other medical conditions and then referred her to a CBT-I specialist for a course of treatment. Agatha contacted Faith, the practitioner recommended by her GP, but she had unfortunately missed the start of the current group programme, which was now halfway through. Since she felt that she needed to be alert during the day to look after her sister, Agatha opted for private sessions, which she could commence immediately.

This involved six fortnightly sessions spread over ten weeks, with each treatment lasting an hour. The programme consisted of assessment, sleep education, relaxation techniques, implementation of a new sleep pattern, maintenance of a sleep log, feedback discussions and guidance, continuous monitoring of sleep pattern, and incremental adjustments made to the sleep pattern as goals were achieved and targets revised.

Agatha was both amazed and delighted by the success of the programme, and her only regret was that she had not embarked on the treatment years earlier. In the couple of years since Agatha's CBT-I treatment, she has noticed a marked improvement in her energy levels and general health, and she no longer falls prey to every cold or bug. Furthermore, Agatha regards her new lifestyle as an unexpected bonus, since she now takes time to wind down in the evening and relishes the end of the day when she can look forward to a deep bath, relaxing read and a restful night's sleep.

Seeing a specialist practitioner in CBT-I is the best way forward; however, if you do not have access to this service or have to endure a considerable wait before starting treatment, here is a brief deconstruction of the CBT-I programme. To follow self-help guidance requires a very high level of motivation and discipline, but it is not impossible, particularly if you can recruit the support of your sleeping partner, should you have one.

Before embarking upon this programme it is *imperative* that you have thoroughly understood how sleep happens, since the educational element concerning the circadian alerting system and sleep drive provides you with essential knowledge that will enable you to change your attitude towards sleep. If you were to see a CBT-I practitioner, they would spend considerable time in explaining the importance of attitude, lifestyle and sleep routine in achieving your aim of sound, reliable sleep.

The more relaxed you can be about your sleep problem, the faster you will overcome it. I know that it is far from easy not to get upset in the middle of the night when you can't sleep and you know that you have a busy day ahead. For this reason, a CBT-I practitioner would teach you relaxation techniques and strategies to help you calm a racing mind, to enable you to remain unflustered if sleep eludes you. Your ability to put into practice the relaxation techniques discussed in chapter 9 will prove useful. The practitioner would also help you to ascertain your sleep requirements by taking a detailed history of your lifestyle and work demands. Your *ideal sleep target* (IST) is unique since everyone varies in the amount of sleep they need; however, it is essential that you allow sufficient time to sleep to meet your individual requirements.

 The aim of CBT-I is to enable an individual to achieve, as far as is practicable, regular, quality sleep. Bear in mind that everyone's sleep needs (or IST) vary over their lifetime, and longer sleep does not necessarily equate to better sleep. The hallmark of quality sleep is when the sleeper feels adequately refreshed and is able to take their sleep at a time that meets their lifestyle requirements. It is unhelpful to compare yourself with others since, as we have already discussed, some of us are by nature of an owl-like disposition, while others are more lark-ish, perhaps in more ways than one!

Some of us are genetically wired to require more sleep to function efficiently, in the same way that our appetites vary. In addition, age and physical demands further dictate our sleep quota needs. A day's hiking and camping are likely to be more soporific than a sedentary day in the office. Similarly, young children are encouraged to exert their energies in the playground or park in the correct hope that it will elicit an undisturbed night's sleep for the parents.

DIY CBT-I

If you suffer from insomnia, then try the following procedure.

First, visit your doctor to rule out any physical causes for your difficulty in sleeping. Implement the facilitate sleep regimen (see p. 159) to address any problems with your current lifestyle and establish the smart bedtime routine (see p. 165) to give yourself the best chance of a sound night's sleep.

Keep a sleep log for at least one week to monitor your sleep pattern. Use the blank log on p. 198 as a template.

The longer you can keep your log going the better, to gain a more accurate picture of your sleep patterns; two weeks of observation would be ideal. However, to simplify the explanation, I have based the guidance on one week only. By recording the time you spend in bed from 'lights out' to the time you get up each morning, you will establish your *potential sleep time* (PST). So, if you switch off the light at 11pm and get up regularly each day when the alarm goes off at 7am, your PST will be eight hours per night or 56 hours per week. Please note that eight hours is a nominal figure, and the sleep requirements of healthy adults will fluctuate considerably both above and below eight hours.

Now record, to the best of your ability, how much time you actually sleep each night. Say, for example, one night it takes you an hour before you fall asleep, having turned off the light at 11pm. This time you spend lying awake is called the *sleep onset latency* (SOL). In the same night, you then wake up at 4.30am and do not get back to sleep until 6am. This 1.5 hours spent awake is called the *interim sleep latency* (ISL). You then wake up at 7am when your alarm goes off. The SOL plus the ISL equals the *sleep debt* (SD), which when subtracted from your PST gives you your *actual sleep time* (AST).

In this example, PST – SD = AST, that is 8 hours – 2.5 hours = 5.5 hours. We can calculate the *sleep efficiency* (SE) as AST divided by PST, expressed as a percentage (expressed here by multiplying by 100): 5.5 ÷ 8 × 100 = 68.75%.

Once you have recorded each night's sleep over the week, add all your AST figures together and divide this total by seven to establish your *average sleep* (AS). You may find that some nights were better or worse than others. It is extremely helpful if you can identify why a particular night's sleep was worse, as this will help you to understand your poor sleep triggers. Once you have identified these, you can work towards avoiding or defusing them. For example, was it a very late, heavy meal, the loud barking of a dog or maybe worry about an important work deadline?

Potential sleep time (PST) is the time available for sleeping between lights out and the alarm going off, which should be equivalent to your ideal sleep target (IST).

Sleep onset latency (SOL) is the amount of time it takes a person to fall asleep from lights out.

Interim sleep latency (ISL) is the time spent awake after having initially fallen asleep.

Sleep debt (SD) is the total time spent awake: SOL plus ISL.

Actual sleep time (AST) is the total time spent asleep.

Sleep efficiency (SE) is the percentage of AST to PST.

If your sleep efficiency is above 90 per cent, this is generally considered to be a good night's sleep. However, the most important factor to keep in mind is whether you feel sufficiently well rested. Losing 10 per cent of sleep for one person may have little impact on their alertness during the day, whereas another person might feel very tired and sluggish. The key is to take the necessary steps to address sleep deprivation when it is causing a negative impact on your life.

Let us look at an example sleep log to illustrate how this is done.

April's sleep log

Day	Hours of sleep (AST)	Poor sleep triggers
Monday	5.5	
Tuesday	3.25	Drank too much alcohol
Wednesday	6.75	
Thursday	2	Worried about tomorrow's work appraisal
Friday	1.5	Watched a thriller and felt very anxious
Saturday	4	
Sunday	5	
Week's total	28	
Average sleep (AS) Week's total divided by 7 days	4	
Sleep efficiency	50%	

This example reveals that April's sleep efficiency is only 50 per cent, since she only slept for 28 hours of the potential 56 hours of sleep. She has also accumulated a sleep debt of 28 hours (PST 56 – AST 28 = SD 28).

Now comes the rub, the really hard bit, which is known as *sleep restriction* (SR). To establish a regular sleep schedule, you must not spend longer in bed each night than your AS figure until you have achieved a minimum of 90 per cent sleep efficiency for at least one week. This creates a powerful link in the brain that bed means sleep. It does not matter how exhausted you feel, you must restrict your sleep to the allocated times and not deviate. After achieving a minimum of 90 per cent sleep efficiency for an entire week, add an additional fifteen minutes to your potential daily sleep time. This cycle should be continued until you reach your ideal sleep target.

At this stage, April must face the difficult choice about when she aims to secure these precious four hours of sleep. She can decide to go to bed at 3am and continue to rise at 7am, or she can continue to go to bed at 11pm but have to get up at 3am (or any permutation in between). You can imagine how difficult it is to discipline yourself to get up at 3am when the alarm goes off, rousing you from a potentially very deep sleep.

You must constantly keep in mind that this is a tried and tested technique that works by reprogramming the brain. So, although this can feel like a form of torture – and in many ways it is, since sleep deprivation (a longer duration of sleep restriction) has been used in this capacity – it truly is worth the short-term pain for the long-term gain. In fact this is a useful mantra, which you can repeat to yourself as a way of self-encouragement in the loneliness of the small hours:

I will tolerate short-term pain for long-term gain.

Now, continuing with April's progress, her target over the next seven days will be to sleep for a *minimum* of 25.2 hours. This minimum comes from working out her 90 per cent sleep efficiency number; in this case 28 hours – 2.8 hours (which is 10 per cent of 28) = 25.2. April must also not exceed 100 per cent of her AS figure and must set herself a maximum of 28 hours overall or four hours on any individual night. The harsh reality of this is that even if April only sleeps for half an hour on one night, she cannot compensate for it on the following night and must stick to four hours maximum. If her 90 per cent minimum target is not achieved (25.2 hours), then April must continue the next week (and so forth) until she achieves this goal.

 It could well have escaped your notice that the smart bedtime routine requires you to leap out of bed if you are not asleep within fifteen minutes and go to another room until you start to feel sleepy.

This same technique applies to CBT-I and is part of your sleep restriction quota. (I did suggest that this was not for the faint-hearted!) It really does require a huge amount of self-discipline to evict yourself from your cosy bed early in the morning during the depths of winter to go into another room should you find that you have woken up prematurely and cannot get back to sleep within fifteen minutes. Prepare for this eventuality with an electric heater and a pre-made flask of a warm, milky drink to ease the pain.

Once the goal has been achieved, April will then add an extra fifteen minutes of sleep per day to her next sleep target, meaning she is now allowed to sleep for a maximum of 4.25 hours per night and 29.75 hours per week. Since April opted to go to bed at 2am and rise at 6am, she has decided to add this extra fifteen minutes to the start of her sleep schedule – so she will now go to bed at 1.45am and will still rise at 6am. This pattern will continue, with the incremental daily addition of fifteen extra minutes per week (or until 90 per cent sleep efficiency has been achieved), until eventually April is able to sleep the full eight hours she deems sufficient to enable her to feel well rested and refreshed when she gets up each morning.

If we assume that April successfully achieves each weekly target to perfection without having to repeat a week (treating 'perfection' as anything greater than 90 per cent of sleep efficiency), from the point that her average sleep time is established as four hours per night (28 hours per week), she will achieve her ideal sleep target in seventeen weeks. To see how April progresses from 50 per cent sleep efficiency to over 90 per cent of her ideal sleep target of 58 hours per week, let's break it down by each week.

April's CBT-I sleep schedule

Week	Hours of sleep per night	Hours of sleep per week
1	4	28
2	4.25	29.75
3	4.5	31.5
4	4.75	33.25
5	5	35
6	5.25	36.75
7	5.5	38.5
8	5.75	40.25
9	6	42
10	6.25	43.75
11	6.5	45.5
12	6.75	47.25
13	7	49
14	7.25	50.75
15	7.5	52.5
16	7.75	54.25
17	8	56

This table shows that in roughly four months, someone can progress from 50 per cent sleep efficiency to 100 per cent. Of course, this would be the ideal outcome; to pass through every single week seamlessly achieving the target will not be the case for everyone. Also keep in mind that April's new sleep schedule would be deemed a resounding success even if she only managed 50 hours and 24 minutes sleep per week, that is 90 per cent of her weekly PST of 56 hours.

Summary of CBT-I steps

1. Keep a sleep log to establish your potential sleep time, actual sleep time, average sleep time and any triggers that might cause poor sleep.

2. Stabilize your sleep pattern by achieving a minimum sleep efficiency of 90 per cent each week.

3. Increase your potential sleep time by fifteen minutes until it equals your ideal sleep target.

Sleep log template

Day	Hours of sleep (AST)	Poor sleep triggers
Monday		
Tuesday		
Wednesday		
Thursday		
Friday		
Saturday		
Sunday		
Week's total		
Average sleep (AS) Week's total divided by 7 days		
Sleep efficiency		

As discussed at the beginning of this book, quality sleep forms the bedrock (no pun intended) for how well you will be able to perform while awake. Do not accept a poor sleep pattern as something that you will just have to live with; with help and determination, quality sleep can be re-established, which in turn will greatly enhance your positive well-being.

Final word

Be yourself; everyone else is already taken.

Oscar Wilde

I hope that I have managed to convey that improving and maintaining positive well-being is made up of many components, including looking after your physical body with proper nutrition, exercise, relaxation and sleep. It is also important that you nurture a healthy mind by keeping negative thinking in check and applying the techniques discussed within to challenge damaging behaviours. By harnessing your ability to manipulate your own biology by increasing vagal tonality, and limiting destructive anxiety by inducing a state of rest and digest, as opposed to fight or flight, you will be well on your way to achieving this goal.

 Adopt the SERENE approach to improve your positive well-being.

Sleep well
Eat sensibly
Relax frequently
Exercise regularly
Nurture a healthy mind
Enjoy life and all its challenges

Equally, I trust that I have successfully emphasized the message that being true to yourself by following your principles, values, dreams and aspirations is absolutely vital to maximize your potential and become all that you can be. This can be achieved by offering yourself the core conditions as enshrined in the person-centred approach (see chapter 3) and ensuring that your emotional needs are recognized and met as described in the human givens approach (see chapter 4).

Being true to yourself, that is being authentic, is not only less demanding, since your energies are not wasted on second guessing how you should be, but is also a highly-valued and admirable attribute, which is appreciated by those around you. Research has shown that we are far more comfortable in the company of people that we perceive as genuine rather than being with those with whom we do not know where we stand. Thus being genuine is a win-win situation; it is an economical and effective way to live for you and provides security for those with whom you interact.

As a trainer of psychotherapists, I often include the following exercise as part of their personal development training. As you continue in your own personal development towards positive well-being, try it out.

Imagine that you are 99 years old and lying on your deathbed, when your much-loved great grandchild asks you: 'Before you go, please tell me how I should live my life.'

You now have only one minute to write down your advice. Make sure that you time yourself and keep what you have to say within those 60 seconds. Do it right now, since mulling over and planning your response will defeat the point of the exercise. There must be a sense of immediate urgency.

Now read back the guidance you have recorded for your great grandchild and ask yourself: are you living your *own* life in accordance with that advice? If you are, that is excellent news, but if not then I urge you to challenge why not. You might argue that you love your great grandchild more than you love yourself and that they deserve the best that life can afford, whereas you do not. If this is the case, this double standard needs to be addressed, as low self-esteem will definitely impact your ability to enjoy positive well-being. Always remember that the most important relationship you have in life is the one you have with yourself. If you cannot value, accept and appreciate yourself, you will never be able to love another with all your being. In addition, you will provide a hopeless role model for those you care about, since what you do is more powerful than what you say.

Read back your own advice and start immediately to put steps in place to 'walk the talk' and live the life you have just described. By putting into action the practices contained in this book you will be on the right track to fulfilling this goal. Remember that seeking to improve your positive well-being is not a selfish pursuit, as it is an enriching experience both for you and for all those around you. A contented and fulfilled person is like a glowing fire, which spreads light, warmth and comfort to everyone in its sphere. So lead by example to empower yourself and others.

I wish you every success in grabbing life by the horns and shaking it until the pips squeak. After all, we only get one shot at this; so make sure that it counts and fully enjoy the life you live.

Useful contacts

UK

Alcoholics Anonymous
Tel: 08457 769 555
www.alcoholics-anonymous.org.uk

Anxiety UK
Tel: 08444 775 774
Email: info@anxietyuk.org.uk
www.anxietyuk.org.uk

Young Minds
Tel: 08088 025 544
www.youngminds.org.uk

Mind
Tel: 03001 233 393
www.mind.org.uk

National Institute for Health Care Excellence
www.nice.org.uk

British Association for Behavioural and Cognitive Psychotherapies
Tel: 01617 054 304
www.babcp.com

British Association for Counselling and Psychotherapy
Tel: 01455 883 300
www.bacp.co.uk

British Psychological Society
Tel: 01162 549 568
www.bps.org.uk

Patricia Furness-Smith
Tel: 01494 766 246
www.maturus.co.uk

Eating Disorders Support
Tel: 01494 793 223
www.eatingdisorderssupport.co.uk

National Counselling Society
Tel: 08708 503 389
www.nationalcounsellingsociety.org

Human Givens Publishing
www.humangivens.com

The Mental Health Foundation
Tel: 02078 031 100
www.mentalhealth.org.uk

No Panic
Tel: 08449 674 848
Email: ceo@nopanic.org.uk
www.nopanic.org.uk

Relate
Tel: 0300 100 1234
www.relate.org.uk

The Sleep Council
Tel: 0800 017 7923
www.sleepcouncil.com

Guided Relaxation Resources
Email: info@widenmind.com
www.widenmind.com

Depression UK
Email: info@depressionuk.org
www.depressionuk.org

The British Association for the Person-Centred Approach
www.bapca.org.uk

See Me Scotland
Tel: 01315 166 819
www.seemescotland.org.uk

Counselling and Psychotherapy in Scotland
Tel: 01786 475 140
www.cosca.org.uk

Australia
Australian Association for Cognitive and Behaviour Therapy
www.aacbt.org

Australian Psychological Society
Tel: (03) 8662 3300 or 1800 333 497
www.psychology.org.au

Canada
Canadian Mental Health Association
www.cmha.ca

The Canadian Association of Cognitive and Behavioural Therapies
www.cacbt.ca/en

Canadian Psychological Association
Tel: 613 237 2144
www.cpa.ca

Anxiety Disorders Association of Canada
Tel: 1 888 223 2252 or 1 514 484 0504
Email: contactus@anxietycanada.ca
www.anxietycanada.ca

Ireland
Irish Health
www.irishhealth.com

Psychological Society of Ireland
Tel: 01 472 0105
www.psihq.ie

New Zealand
New Zealand Psychological Society
Tel: +64 4 473 4884
www.psychology.org.nz

South Africa
Psychological Society of South Africa
Tel: 011 486 3322
www.psyssa.com

**South African National Association of Practicing
Psychologists**
Email: info@sanapp.co.za
www.sanapp.co.za

The South African Depression and Anxiety Group
Tel: 011 234 4837 or 0800 567 567 (emergency out of hours)
www.sadag.org

Selfgrow Development Group
Tel: 021 555 4248
www.selfgrow.co.za

USA
Mental Fitness, Inc.
www.normal-life.org

American Psychological Association
Tel: (202) 336 5500 or (800) 374 2721
www.apa.org

Acknowledgements

I would like to express my deepest appreciation to 'the Venezuelans'. You have been utterly wonderful – deluging me in an avalanche of unconditional love and support. Your caring, empathy and generosity has been superlative and I will be forever grateful that I have been blessed by having you in my life. In addition, I would like to acknowledge my dearest and very special friends and members of my family for all their kindness, practical support and always being there for me. I have been greatly moved by your loyalty and thoughtfulness; so many of you have gone the extra mile, which has touched me deeply. A special mention must go to the wonderful young friends I have inherited. Darling M-J, Fresh, Alpine-John, Ant and Dec, Mr and Mrs D-B and son, Vetinary K, Ascot K and P, the Midgets and the rest of the gang. I love you for the devotion you have shown towards those I love so deeply.

As always, my gratitude goes to all the team at Icon Books; you really are a delightful organization to work with. Specific thanks go to my editor, Kiera Jamison. I enjoyed finding in you a fellow closet word pedant and I appreciated the banter and the excellent support you have given me. Thank you to Mark Ecob whose book jacket designs were subjected to a straw poll in which the hammock won a landslide victory. I am grateful to my most diligent indexer, Jonathan Burd, and hawk-eyed copyeditor, Sara Bryant.

It goes without saying that I would never have met my deadline without the encouragement, humour, pep-talks, hugs and unflagging love and devotion which the two leading men in my life, K and S, never fail to provide for me. Finally Buffy, although this book is dedicated to you, I still want to thank you for 30 fabulous years. You have been a joy and inspiration and, like your father and brother, have helped to shape me into the person I have become. It is not hard to have an attitude of gratitude when surrounded with so much love.

Index

accidents 143–4
actor 48
actual sleep time (AST) 190–1
adenosine 148
advanced sleep phase 176
afternoon apathy syndrome (AAS)
        171–2
Agassi, Andre 36–7
age, and diet 106–7
agitation 47–8
alcohol, impact on sleep 162–4
alpha waves 124, 152, 154
anorexia nervosa 103, 114
antibodies 83
apathy 81
approval, of others 26–7, 31, 34,
        36–7
arousal, control 50–4
attitude 67–89
        adventurous 80
        of gratitude 69–70
authenticity 200
autogenics 128–9
autonomic nervous system (ANS)
        49–50
        see also enteric nervous system;
        parasympathetic nervous system;
        sympathetic nervous system
average sleep (AS) 191

baths 167, 171
bed 166
beta waves 152, 153
biofeedback 185
blood pressure, high 107, 108, 127
'blue sky thinking' 137

Bocelli, Andrea 9
body image, food and 102–3
body mass index (BMI) 105
brain, development 147
brainwaves 124, 152–4, 181
breakfast 109
breathing
        7/11 136
        deep abdominal 60–1, 134–5
        when exercising 96
bright light therapy (BLT) 181–2
Brothers, Joyce 137
bulimia nervosa 56, 114
Bulwer-Lytton, Edward George 1
burn-out 44–5, 81
Byron, Lord 144

caffeine 159–60, 174
calcium intake 107
calories 104–5
CBT-I see cognitive behavioural
        therapy for insomnia
central nervous system (CNS) 49,
        159
central sleep apnoea 176–7
challenges, accepting 81–3
Chandler, Raymond 144
chanting 63–4, 138–9
Churchill, Winston 172
circadian alerting signal 148–9, 188
circadian disorders 176, 181
circadian rhythms 149
cognitive behavioural therapy for
        insomnia (CBT-I) 185–98
        case study 186–7
        DIY 189–97

cognitive distortions 87
collectivism 11
   individualism versus 13–14
comfort eating 113
communication, lack of real 121
conditions of worth (COW) 26–30,
         33, 34, 37
conformity 11–12
congruence 31–3
conscientious objectors 27
contacts 203–7
continuous positive airway pressure
         (CPAP) 182
core conditions 37, 200
cortisol 83, 94, 135, 164
cranial nerves 49
culture, and sense of well-being 11
cybersex 121

dancers 130
darkness 166
daydreaming 137
death 144
deep abdominal breathing 60–1,
         134–5
delayed sleep phase 176
delta waves 153, 154
dementia 82
depression 81, 113
dieting 103, 110
disasters 144
dissonance 12
diurnal monophasia 157
dive reflex 61–2
drink, monitoring intake 162
dyslexia 14

eating disorders 56–7, 103, 114
eating well see healthy eating
electroencephalography (EEG) 181
electromyography (EMG) 181
electrooculography (EOG) 181

element, living in your 73–5
emotional needs 39–45, 200
   resources to meet 39–40, 41–2
endocrine hormones 94
endorphins 74–5, 83–4, 113
energy conservation 147
energy homeostasis 114
enteric nervous system (ENS) 50
Epictetus 85
epilepsy 56
eudaemonic well-being 17–23
exercise 91–9
   aerobic 94–5
   benefits 91–2
   designing routine 93–5
   enjoying 96–7
   resistance 94–5
   and sleep 164–5
expectations, brain working on 86,
         89
experiences, focusing on 78–81
external stimuli, dependence on
         120–1

facial immersion 61–2
facilitate sleep regimen (FSR) 157,
         159–65, 184, 189
fibre 106
fight or flight (F or F) response 47,
         48, 50, 59–60, 119
fitness see exercise
flexibility 78
folic acid deficiency 106
food
   and body image 102–3
   monitoring intake 160–2
forgiveness 70–1
Fredrickson, Barbara 57
friendship 41, 71–2
fruits 114
FSR see facilitate sleep regimen
fulfilment, sense of 22

gamma waves 153
gastroesophageal reflux 177
ghrelin 115, 145
gratitude, attitude of 69–70
Griffin, Joe 39
growth 145, 147
guided imagery 129–32

hangover 163
health
    definition 91
    trading in for convenience 97–9
healthy eating 101–15
    age and 106–7
    balancing diet 107–8
    basic measurements for 104–6
    benefits 101
    hydration 110–12
    listening to your body 114–15
    planning meals 108–10
    responding to emotional
        triggers 112–14
heart, protection 83, 111
hedonic well-being 17–23
Hemingway, Ernest 117
Herodotus 119
Hippocrates 23
homeostasis system 114, 149
homosexuality 12
Horace 81
human givens approach (HGA)
    39–45, 58
humour, embracing 83–5
hydration 110–12
hypersomnia 176
hyperventilation 134–5
hypnotherapy 128–9
hypothalamus 149

ideal self 26
ideal sleep target (IST) 188
ill health, incidence 2

immune system, boosting 83, 128,
    143, 145
incongruence 32
indigestion 160
individualism 11, 13
    collectivism versus 13–14
inferiority complexes 35
inner peace 133
insomnia 161, 171, 172–3, 183–98
    acute 184
    chronic 184
    primary 184
    secondary 184
    symptoms 183–4
    treatment options 185–98
        Biofeedback 185
        CBT-I see cognitive
            behavioural therapy for
            insomnia
        multicomponent therapy
            185
insulin 145, 162
interim sleep latency (ISL) 190, 191

James, William 25
Japan 13–14

K-complexes 152, 154
kidney problems 111–12
Kim Jong-un 19
Kok, Bethany 57

L-tryptophan 162
Lao Tzu 5
'larks' 159
laughter 83–5
lavender 171
left-handedness 14–15
leptin 115, 145
life, pace of 120–1
longevity 56, 59, 93, 101
lottery winners 20–1

Maas, James 172
magnesium deficiency 161
Mandela, Nelson 19
Marcos, Imelda 21–2
Mason, John 38
massage 134
medication, for sleep disorders
        177–80
meditation 58–9, 63, 127–8
melatonin 162, 166, 167, 170
melatonin supplements 178
memory 84, 106, 145, 146–7
mental health disorders 1–2
metabolism downshifting 55, 103,
        109, 146, 147
Milton, John 67
mindfulness 58–9, 127–8
mixed nerves 54
monophasic sleep 158
multicomponent therapy 185
muscle relaxation 126–7, 133–4

napping 172–3
narcolepsy 176
nervous system 48–52
    central 49, 159
    see also peripheral nervous
        system
neurons 48, 147, 151, 153
neurotransmitters 50, 113, 147,
        153, 162
niacin 161
nicotine 159
'night owls' 159
nocturnal animals 158
noise 165
non-rapid eye movement (NREM)
        sleep 151–5
    stage one 151–2
    stage three 152–3
    stage two 152

obesity 104
    central 106
objective measures of well-being
        10
obstructive sleep apnoea (OSA)
        181, 182
optimism
    as default stance 85–8
    vagal tonality and 58
organismic self 26, 34
organismic valuing process 30–1
others, investing in 74–6
outdoor activity 97
Owen, Wilfred 27
oxytocin 72, 76

panic attacks 55, 118, 119
paradoxical intention technique
        168
parasomnias 176
parasympathetic nervous system
        (PSNS) 50, 119, 135
    sympathetic nervous system vs.
        51–2
passive muscle relaxation 126–7
Patagonia 158
perfection, lowering standards of
        79–80
periodic limb movement disorder
        176
peripheral nervous system (PNS) 49
    see also autonomic nervous
        system; somatic nervous
        system
person-centred approach (PCA)
        25–38
    how it works 33–7
pessimism 85–7
phenomenological approach 30–1
physical needs 40
placebo effect 59
polyphasic sleep 158

polysensorial approach 130
polysomnogram (PSG) 180–1
Pope, Rosie Swale 77
positive regard 26
potassium deficiency 161
potential sleep time (PST) 190,
    191, 197
poverty 21
power nap 172–3
progressive muscle relaxation
    133–4
prophecy, self-fulfilling 86
PSNS see parasympathetic nervous
    system
puddings 78

rapid eye movement (REM) sleep
    146, 150–1, 163
reflections, positive 88–9
relationships
    intimate 72–3
    valuing 71–3
relaxation 117–39
    control 50–4
    as essential aspect of our nature
        136–9
    exercises 60–4, 125–36
    importance 117–19
    response 119–20
    resting vs. 124
    routes to 124–5
    as skill 122–4
    and sleep 165
    using body to relax mind 133–6
    using mind to relax body
        126–32
resources, to meet emotional needs
    39–40, 41–2
rest and digest (R & D) 47, 48, 118,
    135
resting, relaxation vs. 124
restless legs syndrome 176

rewards 20
rewind technique 87
risks, taking 81–3
Rochefoucauld, Francois de La 117
Rogers, Carl 25–6, 28, 31, 33, 72
rust-out 81

Saint-Exupéry, Antoine de 9, 22
salivation 62–3
salt intake 107, 108
satisfaction, intrinsic/extrinsic 20–1
SBR see smart bedtime routine
sedentariness 98
self
    ideal 26
    organismic 26, 34
self-acceptance 38, 201
self-confidence 35, 137
SERENE approach 199
serenity 133
serotonin 75, 113, 114, 161, 162
Shakespeare, William 143
siesta 158
sigma waves (sleep spindles) 152,
    154
sitting-rising test (SRT) 92–3
sleep
    advice to improve 157–74
    benefits 144–6
    exercise and 164–5
    how it happens 147–9
    how much needed 155–6
    need for 146–7
    relaxation and 165
    stages 150–5
    what it is 143
    see also smart bedtime routine
sleep clinics 180–2, 185
sleep cycle 149–55
sleep debt (SD) 190, 191
sleep deprivation 143–4, 175
sleep diary 185

sleep disorders 175–82
  treatments 177–82
  see also insomnia
sleep drive 148–9, 188
sleep efficiency (SE) 191, 197
sleep hygiene 157
sleep inertia 153, 173
sleep log 189–90, 192–3, 197, 198
sleep onset latency (SOL) 190, 191
sleep restriction (SR) 193–5
sleep spindles 152, 154
smart bedtime routine (SBR) 157,
    165–71, 184, 189, 194
  bedroom use 170
  environment 165–7
  winding down routine 167–70
smoking 159–60
SNS see sympathetic nervous
    system
society, attitudes 11–14
somatic nervous system (SoNS) 49
spinal nerves 49
stimulants, reducing 159–60
stimulus control 168–9
stress
  and brain cells 81
  management 122–3
  mini stress-busters 137–8
  reduction through relaxation
    118–19
stress hormones 83, 118, 135
sugar intake 108
suicide 2–3
suprachiasmatic nucleus (SCN) 149
sympathetic nervous system (SNS)
    50, 135
  parasympathetic nervous system
    vs. 51–2

tai chi 133

technology, addiction to 121
temperature, bedroom 166
Teresa, Mother 21–2
theta waves 152, 154
tiredness
  dealing with during day 171–4
  on the road 173–4
tongue immersion 62–3
tryptophan 114, 161, 162
Tyrrell, Ivan 39

unconditional positive regard 33–7,
    72

vagal manoeuvres 54, 60
vagal tonality 57–8
  and optimistic outlook 58
  power of body in promoting
    59–64
vagus nerve 49, 50, 54–5, 135
  functions 55–6
vagus nerve stimulation (VNS)
    56–7
vegetables 114
ventilation 166–7
Virgil 144
vitamin B deficiency 106
vitamin D 97, 164–5

waist measurement 106
Washington, Booker T. 76
wastage, avoiding 80
water, importance 110–12
Wilde, Oscar 70, 199
winding down routine 167–70
World War I 27
World War II 19–20, 27
worrying 51

yoga 133